Jesus and the Metaphysics of God
One Skeptic's Search for the Truth

Vince Procopio

April 1998

Dorrance Publishing Co
585 Alpha Drive
Pittsburgh, PA 15238
Visit our website at www.dorrancebookstore.com

ISBN: 979-8-8868-3069-9
eISBN: 979-8-8868-3929-6

TABLE OF CONTENTS

PART I
Preface

The year is 1969. I'm a USMC grunt in Vietnam. I'm in a bunker taking a break from the madness of war. In my hands is a book entitled *What is Philosophy*--a Barnes and Noble outline. All my life I was consumed by a raging philosophical fire that demanded to know the meaning of life- mine in particular. Finally, in my hands, there was a formal outline of the metaphysical topics which had haunted me for so long.

I must have been nine or ten years old when the thought occurred to me: "What if there was no God? Then would there be nothing forever and ever?" My good Catholic upbringing biased my thinking towards the presupposition that God created everything.

In later years as I became involved in graduate training in philosophy, I would rephrase the question as: "Why is there something rather than nothing?"

There were so many strands that ran through my thinking. Politically speaking, I am a Libertarian. A partial list of people that have been the most influential in my political thinking would include: Ayn Rand, Nathaniel Branden, Murray Rothbard, David Kelley, Charles Murray, Milton and David Friedman, and Doug Casey. Often accompanying that stream of thought was a belief in atheism.

Within religious context, I'm most sympathetic to the views of Buddhism. It is by far the most psychologically sophisticated of all the major religions.

In the history of religion, Judaism with its long and glorious history is very appealing.

What is my purpose in writing this book? First of all, I wanted this book to be a personal journey of my progress on the spiritual path. Accordingly, the book is written from first person perspective.

Secondly, I refer to myself as a "seeker of truth." I am so saddened when I hear reports about a medium or religious figure in general living in luxury as a result of exploiting the spiritual. I'm so painfully reminded daily that we came into the world penniless and so will our inevitable exit be likewise. As corrupting as money can be, only the Truth can set us free.

Third, I am amazed how tribal we tend to be. For example, if I were a Christian and felt secure in my faith, the first book I would read would be on "atheism." I think understanding the arguments proposed by atheists may strengthen the chosen faith of the believer. So often we become ensconced in our own little tribe. To tread outside its scope brings uncertainty. Familiarity is like a narcotic. It dulls the mind into accepting the familiar.

As I reflect upon my life, I think about how predictable–within broad parameters–life can be. We grow up with certain values and beliefs. As adults, we tend to reflect our parental upbringing, whether or not our parents were responsible role models. How many among us can forsake the powerful effects of our upbringing and come to a set of values that we have freely chosen? This is the road less-traveled.

Finally, as a child I was taught to believe in Jesus–Son of God. As a matter of faith, I implicitly respect anyone who professes a belief in Jesus. I must say that I am thoroughly impressed with the many testimonials from born-again Christians. Life-changing experiences are significant. We know that attitudes and beliefs are relatively permanent. When an experience is transformational, we must listen to what it may teach us.

My task in this book is to approach the subject of Jesus from a historical and empirical framework. If someone believes in Jesus Christ as a matter of faith, then the door is closed to any further inquiry. My intended reader is the skeptic and those with an insatiable curiosity to know more about the many unexamined, religious beliefs inculcated in us during our formative years. I have tried to synthesize the views of many authors from as many sides as I could find. For the past several years, my primary focus has been on the historical evidence for Jesus. All scholars were welcomed. From atheists to skeptics to religious fundamentalists, Christians, non-Christians, scientists, and philosophers. I have tried to sample each perspective. I feel humbled when I look at the many prodigious scholars that have spent a lifetime studying the topic of Jesus. I walk in their shadows. I stand on their shoulders to extend their reach.

For me, this book represents a culmination of a thirty-three year journey. After reviewing the search for Jesus, I wish to broaden the inquiry into the nature of God. I will examine some of the arguments and counterarguments on the existence of God.

Why should you read this book? I'm convinced that my journey has come full circle. As a child, my innocence led me to a strong belief that God created the universe and would balance the scales of justice. While growing up, my skepticism grew. Wisdom and understanding were always one book away. After reading thousands of books, I'm also convinced that the ultimate result of voracious reading is confusion. One doesn't come to God through reason alone. I wish to respect the epistemological limits of reason to make room for faith. It isn't my purpose to undermine faith, but to strengthen it.

I attempted to start this project several months ago. But then another book would come to my attention that I would absolutely have to read. And then another and another... Analogously, I'm reminded of my decision to postpone my purchase of a computer because prices would fall in due time. At some point, the decision had to be made and the first step taken.

Chapter One

Imagine that a group of fifty people report seeing the presence of a UFO. The individuals appear highly credible and sincere. Furthermore, they represent a cross-section of occupations.

Their stories appear incredibly uniform. A saucer-shaped object appeared in the hills at varying distances from where the individuals lived. They observed the spacecraft landing. Upon landing, the craft's occupants were observed disembarking. The profile of their appearance was described as approximately four feet in height with disproportionately large heads. Further, a faint luminescence emanated from their bodies.

Question: How believable would such a story be? Let's assume further that it was later discovered that the fifty diverse people who observed the reported UFO were also members of a UFO society. How credible would the story now be?

I use this admittedly crude analogy to show the limited and partisan nature of the Gospel accounts. Jesus was a Jew. The Gospels were written by fellow Jews—believers in the faith. It would serve the Christian Apologetic's cause if he could address the proof of Jesus's claims based upon non-Christian sources. Unfortunately, as A.N. Wilson points out, the totality of non-Christian sources would amount to a postcard.[1] Further compounding the problem is that of the two main non-Christian writers of the Common Era (CE), Josephus and Tacitus. Their writing, as passed down to us, may have been "contaminated." In particular, *Testimonium Flavianum* in what is referred to as *The Antiquities of the Jews*, written in AD 93, Josephus writes, "About this time there lived Jesus, a wise man [if indeed one ought to call him a man]. For he was one who brought surprising feats and was a teacher of such peoples as accept the truth gladly. He won over many Jews and many of the Greeks. [He was the Messiah]."[2] The bracketed paragraphs are in dispute. But even taken as authentic, I find the cursory reference to be unconvincing. When we look at all the miraculous feats that are mentioned in the Gospels and the impact of Jesus upon the Jewish society, quoting from Josephus is self-defeating if the aim is to bolster the divinity of Jesus.

Hence, we are left with the writings of Paul and the four Gospels as the primary source of material. Again, it must be mentioned that the aim of Christian Apologetics is to establish that Jesus is the Christ. This search is intrinsically flawed. We know today that the issue of experimental bias can contaminate any experiment. That is, double blind studies are employed where both the subject and the experimenter are "blind" to who is receiving the treatment.

I'm not just impressed with the historical evidence of young Jewish children reciting the Torah by memory as evidence of the reliability of the Gospels. The point is that if you are a believer in a faith, your writings will be distorted. It doesn't make any difference how objective you try to be. We know the effect of the subconscious is subtle but real.

Many Christian believers try to evade this central issue of contamination by positing that the Gospel writers were inspired by God. That addendum, while satisfactory on one level, has its own set of problems. How can we account for the different and irreconcilable gospel accounts? My response to this is that before we invoke the metaphysical, we must first exhaust the natural or physical. It simply compounds the problem further to enlist God as the source of reliability. Furthermore, we must look at the Bible through Jewish eyes if we are to fully understand its meaning. In this regard, I am indebted to the writings of Bishop John Shelby Spong for the powerful impact he has had upon me. The Old Testament provides valuable clues of interpretation in understanding the Gospels.

Finally, I would say that I'm also profoundly influenced by the writings of Josh McDowell—the Christian Apologetic.[3] There is little doubt that the transformation of the disciples from quarrelsome cowards to courageous martyrs after the resurrection of Jesus needs explaining. I don't believe that we can dismiss the New Testament as a mere Christian concoction. This would constitute the opposite extreme of treating the Bible as the infallible word of God. It is in the middle path that I believe the truth will be found.

The Origins of the Gospels

I'm extremely suspicious when one faith claims a monopoly of truth. Even the use of the word Bible needs definition. We know that the Hebrew Bible is different than the Christian and different than the Protestant Bible. The Protestant Bible excludes a number of books from the Old Testament that have come to be called the Apocrypha.[4]

Burton Mack writes, "It is, however, the New Testament part of the Bible that makes a Christian Bible, and it is the Christian Bible that has influenced our culture."[5]

When examining the Gospels, it should be noted that they were written anonymously.[6] Burton Mack notes that, "...in the early period of collecting lore, interpreting teachings, and trying out new ideas fit for the novel groupings, many minds, voices and hands were in on the drafting of written materials. No one thought to take credit for writing down community property even though creativity is everywhere in evidence."[7]

It wasn't until 180 CE that the names attached to the Gospels first appeared.[8] Furthermore, the number of Gospels was more than four. The Christian hierarchy rendered one of many decisions as to which were authoritative, and which were apocryphal.

I concur with historian E.P. Sanders' analysis that most of the Apocryphal Gospels that were dismissed had little relevance to the life of Jesus.[9] My main point is to suggest that whatever the outcome, this was a church decision.

We know that the destruction of Jerusalem by the Romans occurred around 70 CE. The only Gospel that is generally considered to have been written before that event was Mark. The general range is from 64 to 72 AD.[10] Paul died in 64 CE. Hence, we can be sure that his writings are the earliest available testimony we have.

The last written Gospel was John–somewhere in the 9th century CE. The Matthew and Luke historical sequence is a little bit more contentious, ranging between 75 CE and 85 CE. Bishop Spong dates Matthew between 80 and 82 CE- the best guess among scholars.[11] In addition, he dates Luke's writings in the ninth decade.[12] However, as I shall shortly argue, it may be more consistent to reverse the order of Matthew and Luke. The historical sequence is more important than Christians believe. If one accepts this historical evolution as accurate, then we can immediately dismiss the commonly held notion that the New Testament is the inerrant Word of God. The reason that this dramatic conclusion is permitted is because we can compare the texts to show how each writer changed the story to accommodate his particular audience and circumstances. As I will show later, comparing and juxtaposing the different texts yields valuable clues in deciphering the mental state of the author.

Another way to ascertain the historical sequence of the Gospels is by examining the contents of each of the writers. The operating hypothesis is that as traditions developed, more embellishment would be added to the Gospel stories.

Of the 664 verses in Mark, Matthew includes 606 in his narrative.[13] Hence, it would be difficult to believe that Matthew was writing independent of Mark. In addition, approximately one-half of the Book of Mark is incorporated into Luke.[14]

These three Gospels are referred to as the Synoptics. John is the most independent and original of the four.

Let's take an example as to how tradition was embellished. Who did the women see at the tomb? According to Mark, it was a young man in a white robe. According to Matthew, it was an angel of the Lord. In Luke, we now have "two men in clothes that gleamed like lightning. And in John we have two angels. Hence, this evolution of embellishment would create the order of Mark, Luke, Matthew, and John.

A: Gospels as Midrash

I'm intrigued by Bishop Spong's analysis that the Gospels were midrashic interpretations of Old Testament scriptures. That is, using the Old Testament to give meaning to the writings of the New Testament. What makes this hypothesis so appealing is the Gospel writers themselves. In Corinthians 1:15, Paul writes, "For what I received I passed on to you as of first importance that Christ died for our sins according to the Scriptures..."

All four Gospels have Jesus entering Jerusalem riding a donkey (Mark 11:1, Luke 19:35, Matthew 21:1-9, and John 12:12-15).

Now, why is this significant? If we go back to Zechariah–the penultimate book of the Old Testament–we read these words: "Rejoice greatly, O Daughter of Zion shout, Daughter of Jerusalem. See your King comes to you righteous and having salvation, gentle and riding on a donkey, on a colt, the foal of a donkey" (Zechariah 9:9).

There are many other prophecies that could be chosen. But this particular one is illustrative. In addition, it has the merit of multiple attestations, i.e., confirmation by more than one source; unlike, the virgin birth stories which are mentioned only in Luke and Matthew.

What do the prophecies mean? If we are to be true to the cause, the operating principle must always be, "Exhaust the physical before evoking the metaphysical." That is, let us seek out plausible natural explanations before deciding on extra physical alternatives.

There are at least two hypotheses that present themselves:

1. Certain events in the life of Jesus were prophecies recorded by the Old Testament writers (the metaphysical hypothesis).

2. The accounts of Jesus were applied retrospectively after his death.

According to John Dominic Crossan, "... Jesus's first followers knew almost nothing whatsoever about the details of his crucifixion, death or burial. What we have now in those passion accounts is not history remembered but prophecy historicized."[15] Crossan adds that by prophecy, "I do not mean texts, events, or persons that predicted or foreshadowed the future... I mean such units sought out backwards, as it were sought after the events of Jesus's life were already known and his followers declared that the texts from the Hebrew Scriptures had been written with him in mind."[16]

We know that the years 29-33 CE [17] constitute the best guess for the death of Jesus. We said earlier that the Gospels were written somewhere between 64 CE and 99 CE. That means that thirty-one years at a minimum, had elapsed from the time that Jesus died to the first written Gospel account. Would it not be plausible to believe that the writer of Mark, fully cognizant of the predictions in Zachariah, had the book open for reference in trying to understand the meaning of Jesus? I find this to be a perfectly reasonable explanation for the accuracy of prophecy.

On the other hand, it would be a wide stretch to invoke a metaphysical explanation. The compelling point would be to show that Gospel writers were ignorant of the book of Zachariah. But since they quote the relevant passage, ignorance can't serve as an explanation.

When reading the New Testament, the crucial question is not to ask, "Did it really happen?" but "What does it mean?"[18]

In the fable of the boy who cried wolf, the moral point of the story is not to ask, "Did it really happen?" but rather, what message can be sifted from the details. Its essence is not lost despite its redundant and simple style.

That the New Testament has elements of midrash is undeniable, in my opinion. However, the crucial question is this: Is the New Testament, in general, a midrashic attempt at interpretation? Or can we allow degrees of midrash within a historical context?

Bishop Spong is a sincere and honest man. I think about his enormous courage in dramatically countering the teachings of the Church. Having been brought up as a fundamentalist, he now dismisses any literal interpretation of the Bible, especially the New Testament.

For Spong, the birth narratives, Judas, Joseph–the father of Jesus–the virgin birth, and even the Resurrection can all be dismissed as midrashic interpretations. In the case of Judas, no such historical figure exists. Rather, for Spong, it represents the Jewish nation as a collective.

As Bishop Spong writes, "I do not today regard the details of the gospel tradition as possessing literal truth in any primary way. I do not believe that the Gospels offer us either reliable eyewitness testimony or realistic objective history. I do believe that Gospels are Jewish attempts to interpret a Jewish way of life, the life of a Jewish man in whom transcendence of God was believed to have been experienced in a fresh and powerful encounter."[19]

If the literalism of the Bible can be dismissed as midrash, then many beliefs have to be jettisoned. The implications are enormous. Only an internal battle can do justice to the issues involved.

I want to explore the concept of midrash in greater detail, for within its bosom so many secrets reside. We have seen that the Gospel authors and Paul were Jewish writers. History can best be understood within its social context. We are all creatures of the past. If we understand the culture, we can go back and trace the individual mindset. And conversely, we can proceed from the micro, i.e., the individual, to the macro-society at large.

What was the social context of the Jews at the time of Jesus? The recurring nostalgic theme for the Jews was the kingdom of David, which flourished around 1030 BCE. Unfortunately, in most of the kingdom's history, the Jewish people were oppressed. In times of great suffering, the nostalgia of former glory days was often recalled.

In 596 BCE the city of Jerusalem fell to the Babylonian army. As people began to intermarry, Israel's identity became increasingly threatened. Furthermore, internal revolutions led to the deportation of Israel's elite.

As a means to preserve their national identity during captivity, the priestly leaders devised two prescriptions: (1) the practice of circumcision which had been largely discontinued, and 2) the worship of the Sabbath which would fall on Saturday. Hence, these two features became the distinguishing marks of every Jew.

In 539 BCE, the Babylonians were conquered by Cyrus- the Persian. During this time the Jews were allowed to return to Jerusalem and restore their great temple. For two hundred years, Persian rule proved to be relatively benevolent. However, with the defeat of Darius at the battle of Issus by Alexander the Great, Greek influence was to become widespread.

In 175 BCE, some of the aristocratic priests began introducing a more Hellenistic lifestyle. With the accession of Antiochus IV Epiphanies to the throne, the Jews were forced to violate some of their more basic customs. The temple in Jerusalem was forced to sacrifice to pagan gods. Jews were forced to transgress dietary laws such as the eating of pork. Circumcision was viewed as an abomination of the body. The Sabbath was violated.

This clash of cultural values culminated in the "Maccabean Revolt" resulting in the establishment of the priestly family–the Hasmoneans. For approximately one hundred years until 75 BCE, the Hasmoneans defiantly flourished until it rivaled the kingdom of David in size if not in glory.

At the end of this time, a struggle occurred between two Hasmonean brothers, Hyrcanus II and Aristobulus II. In their struggle for power, each appealed to the support of the Roman army. In 63 BCE, the Roman general Pompey conquered the territory. He discovered that the Sabbath was a good day to fight the Jews. The only serious resistance he discovered occurred at the temple.

Pompey's victory changed the status of the Jewish government into a semi-independent state. As long as the approved ruler supported Roman policies, a high measure of autonomy was afforded.

By the year 37 BCE, Herod was appointed ruler until his death thirty-three years later. Around the year 4 BCE, upon Herod's death, the kingdom was divided among his three sons: Archelaus, Antipas, and Philip. Herod's successors were also called "Herod," just as the name "Caesar" was generalized beyond Julius.

Of the three brothers, Antipas, who governed Galilee and Persia, was the most successful. Generally speaking, he was fairly respective of Jewish law. As a result, relatively few uprisings are reported. Antipas governed for forty-three years until his death in 39 CE.

Archelaus inherited Judea, Samaria, and Idumea. His reign proved to be more troublesome. In 6 CE he was deposed and exiled by Rome. Roman officials were given jurisdiction over the territory. Such officials were given the name of "prefect", of which Pontius Pilate was the most famous. He ruled from 27 AD to 36 AD.

The prefect had a garrison of approximately three thousand troops to handle dissent.[20] Smaller garrisons were located in Jerusalem and in Judea. The legate of Syria was another Roman official actually superior to the prefect. The legate had at his command approximately four legions (25,000 troops) which were commonly used during the holiday festivals to contain the swollen crowds.

It should be noted that the country was in continual ferment. The ongoing oppression of the Jewish nation fed the hope that Yahweh would intervene directly to destroy Israel's enemies.

B: The Social Strata

We know that Roman society was primarily agrarian. The stratification of society was divided into seven strata. At the top stood the ruler and governors. Next came the priestly class. Next came the retainers (military experts to expert bureaucrats). The merchants came next. The peasants constituted the vast majority of the population living barely at the subsistence level. They constituted the common laborers whose primary living was from the land. Next came the artisans–5% of the total– who, even though they had crafts, were considered lower than the peasants. Why? Crossan explains, "Because they were usually recruited and replenished from its dispossessed members."[21] The last rung in the social ladder was occupied by the degraded and expendable classes, constituting as much as 10% of the population. These included the beggars, day laborers, and slaves.

Crossan writes, "If Jesus was a carpenter, therefore, he belonged to the artisan class ... I emphasize that any decision on Jesus's socioeconomic class must be made not in terms of Christian theology but of cross-cultural anthropology ... Furthermore, since between 95%97% of the Jewish state was illiterate at the time of Jesus, it must be presumed that Jesus was also illiterate..."[22]

I find it interesting to contrast these remarks with Mack. "Jesus grew up in Galilee and apparently had some education ... He must have been something of an intellectual, for the teachings of the movements stemming from him are highly charged with penetrating insights and ideas."[23]

Whichever version of Jesus is correct, it is rather obvious that Jesus must have commanded great appeal and charisma. Even the small percentage (17%) of sayings adjudged to be authentic by the Jesus Seminar bespeaks of historical insights and depth.

C: Midrash Examined

Given this historical context, let us go back to the original question of how much of the Bible can be attributed to midrashic expression?

Let me begin with Spong's words, "Midrash is the Jewish way of saying that everything to be reunited in the present must somehow be connected with a second moment in the past. It is the ability to rework an ancient theme in a new context. It is the affirmation of a timeless truth found in the faith journey of a people so that his truth can be experienced anew in every generation."[24]

Spong goes on to note that Joshua–the successor to Moses–was also given credit for parting the water of the Jordan River. I found the symbolism appealing. If you are trying to maintain continuity in the Jewish story, the ability to part waters maintains the theme of God's intervention with his chosen people.

If Moses parted the Red Sea and the prophet Joshua parted the Jordan River, than if Jesus is the greater figure, his deeds must transcend the parting of waters. What then does Jesus part? Spong writes, "The Gospel writers had Jesus begin his public career by walking into the waters of the Jordan River and parting not the waters, but the heaven themselves..."[25]

I find the line of reasoning entirely plausible. But to make the point more compelling, let us look at some parallels between the Old Testament and New Testament.

Old Testament Story	New Testament Parallel
1. The confusion of tongues at the Tower of Babel (Genesis 11:1-9)	1. The confusion of tongues at Pentecost (Acts 2)
2. Killing of Jewish babies by Pharaoh (Exodus 1:22)	2. Killing of Jewish babies by Herod in Bethlehem (Matthew 2:16-18)
3. Moses witnessing God resulting in a radiant face (Exodus 34:29)	3. Jesus's transformation with Moses and Elijah (Mark 9:2-8)
4. The Messiah entering Jerusalem on a donkey (Zechariah 9:9-11)	4. Jesus, the Messiah, entering Jerusalem on a donkey (Matthew 11:2-10; Matthew 21:1-9; Luke 19:28-38)
5. Abraham and Sarah having a child in their old age	5. Zechariah and Elizabeth, parents of John the Baptist, having a child in their old age
6. Guiding star appearing in the births of Abraham, Isaac, and Moses	6. Guiding star appearing in the birth of Jesus
7. Vision of Daniel speaking with Gabriel in the temple	7. Vision of Zechariah speaking with Gabriel in the temple

8. Song of Hannah	8. Song of Mary, Mother of Jesus
9. Story of Samuel in the temple	9. Story of Jesus in the temple
10. Queen of Sheba bringing spices to honor Solomon, King of the Jews (1 Kings 10:1-13)	10. The Three Wise Men bringing gifts to honor the birth of Jesus
11. Joseph betrayed by Judah, one of his eleven brothers.	11. Jesus betrayed by Judas, one of his twelve disciples

The list can be expanded considerably. But I think the examples are sufficient to make the point as to how midrashic interpretations are incorporated in New Testament doctrine. But wait! If prophecy was being manifested in the NT, wouldn't we expect such parallelism and redundancy? As mentioned previously, this is probably one of the weakest arguments used to substantiate the historicity of Jesus. The temporal gap between Jesus's death and the writings of Paul and the other Gospel authors would certainly have provided sufficient time to incorporate the Old Testament's so-called prophecies.

Furthermore, if I may be allowed one excursion at this point, I find it incredulous that despite the fact that Jesus was a Jew, most present-day Jews deny his divinity. Why? If we read the overwhelming majority of NT writings, the prediction was that Jesus would be the next Messiah to occupy the throne of King David. "He will be great and will be called the Son of the Most High. The Lord God will give him the throne of his father David..." (Luke 1:29)

This was certainly the expectation of the Jewish community. If Moses had freed them from the chains of Pharaoh, then surely Jesus—the greater Moses—would free them from bondage of the Romans.

An expanded theme concerning the Messiah comes from the Dead Sea Scrolls where the writers portray two Messiahs: one Davidic and royal; the other Levitical and priestly.[26] However, it should be noted that the common expectation was that Jesus would follow in the footsteps of a king like David.

I want to come back to this point later. For now, I note it as a point of interest.

Returning to the midrashic theme, the central point that we must bear in mind is that midrashic interpretation is a method used to give meaning to certain experiences. Symbols are more powerful than words in capturing the intensity of an experience.

However, there is an epistemological problem in concluding that the NT is all midrash. I'm reminded from my philosophy days of Immanuel Kant. For Kant, there existed what he referred to as noumenal realm. This realm of reality is inaccessible to our consciousness. Our mental categories including our concepts of time and space apply only to the phenomenal realm- that which we do perceive.

Similarly, the chain of causation runs as follows: Experiences ——› Beliefs——› Interpretation——› Synthesis. Let's take the resurrection. The disciples had several experiences of the risen Jesus. This experience was filtered through the beliefs of their faith, namely the OT. An interpretation was made using that filter. As a result, a new set of beliefs emerged.

One of the problems of using this analogy is that there is no precedent for a singular resurrection. There was, however, a commonly held belief in a general resurrection at the end of time. Hence, it would prove difficult to interpret an experience which was unprecedented in history.

Furthermore, the main problem that I see with this perspective is that it substitutes a metaphysics further removed from historicity. Midrashic interpretations are three levels removed from reality (belief, interpretation, and synthesis). Hence, they ensconce us further into the realm of metaphysics. And ultimately, faith. In the realm of faith, each individual's beliefs are as good as any other.

However, we cannot simply dismiss the NT as mere midrash. For to be sure the Bible does contain facts that are grounded in history. There are many prominent historians such as Sir William Ramsay who attest to the accuracy of the geography,social structure and antiquities as noted in the Book of Acts.

The noted historian E.P. Sanders lists the following facts about Jesus which are beyond dispute. It is worth quoting this passage in its entirety:

1. "Jesus was born circa. 4 BCE, near the time of death of Herod the Great;
2. He spent his childhood and early adult years in Nazareth, a Galilean village;
3. He was baptized by John the Baptist;
4. He called disciples;

> 5. He taught in towns, villages, and countrysides of Galilee (apparently not in the cities);
>
> 6. He preached the Kingdom of God;
>
> 7. About the year 30 he went to Jerusalem for Passover;
>
> 8. He created a disturbance in the temple area;
>
> 9. He had a final meal with the disciples;
>
> 10. He was arrested and interrogated by Jewish authorities, specifically the high priest;
>
> 11. He was executed on the orders of the Roman prefect, Pontius Pilate;
>
> 12. ...His disciples at first fled;
>
> 13. They saw him (in what sense is not certain) after his death;
>
> 14. As a consequence, they believed that he would return to have found the kingdom;
>
> 15. They formed a community to await his return and sought to win others to faith in him as God's Messiah."[27]

I think that Sanders's analysis is one of the most reliable and objective based upon the available evidence. To the extent that the NT yields accurate accounts confirmed by empirical, historical methods, then the task of dismissing its pages as mere midrash proves difficult.

Perhaps the truth, as is so often the case, is found in the middle. That is, the NT does contain elements of midrash and historical facts.

In *The Historical Reliability of the Gospels*, Craig Blomberg makes a similar conclusion. "No entire gospel is a commentary on any portion of earlier scriptures, but small sections seem to be. No gospel very closely resembles the ancient Jewish works specifically called Midrash, but midrashic methods of interpretation seem to appear from time to time within the evangelists' narratives."[28]

If we accept this position, we can then subject the contents to critical analysis. The primary aim is to separate the wheat of historical truth from the chaff of religious accretions.

Chapter Two: The Letters of Paul

It is upon the bedrock of Jesus's Resurrection that Christianity depends. If the story can be made coherent across the different accounts, then I believe that the Christian faith can be strengthened. Let's take each writer in turn.

As I mentioned earlier, Paul was writing circa 55 AD, approximately twenty-two years after the death of Jesus. The most famous passage we have is contained in Corinthians 15:3-8: "For I delivered to you as of first importance, that Christ died for our sins according to the Scriptures, and He was buried, and that He appeared to Cephas, then to the twelve. After that He appeared to more than five hundred brethren at one time, most of whom remain until now, but some have fallen asleep; then He appeared to James, then to all the apostles. And last of all as it were to one untimely born, He appeared to me also."

When did this event occur? According to Professor James Dunn, "Paul was converted within two or three years of Jesus's death, perhaps as little as eighteen months after the last reports of Jesus being seen alive after his death."[1]

What I find curious about this passage is that if the Resurrection was a physical event, then Jesus would've continued to exist for at least eighteen months after his crucifixion. No other Gospel writer makes this claim. Luke has Jesus appearing for up to forty days after his resurrection (Luke 24:36-51).

The question that arises is: where did Jesus live during this lengthy period? And how are we to understand "spiritual body"? I believe that there is a plausible case for distinguishing spiritual from physical body. I find the passages starting with Corinthians 42 to be fairly impressive on this point. "The body that is shown is perishable, it is raised imperishable."

Someone can object and claim that these passages refer to the general resurrection and not specifically to the resurrection of Jesus. Fair enough! I accept the point. But it is clear that the resurrected body of Jesus was different than the body assumed before his death.

In Luke 24:13-24 it is clear that the physical body is different. Two men encounter Jesus on the road to Emmaus. What I find so unusual about this story is that Jesus was not initially recognized. In some way, his appearance was distorted to render him unrecognizable. The passage is more revealing in what it doesn't say. It doesn't say that Jesus was translucent, had a halo, or was distinguishable in any non-physical way.

The point is repeated in John 20:10-18. Mary Magdalene also fails to recognize Jesus in the beginning. However, contrast this theme with Matthew 28:8-10, where Jesus is immediately recognized.

It is fair to say that despite these contradictions that the resurrected body of Jesus was different from his natural body prior to his death. In trying to understand that difference, our journey would take us into a realm of speculation. However, I will venture forth a hypothesis before I close this chapter on Paul.

Note further what Paul omits in his writings. There are no references to empty tombs, Joseph of Arimathea, disappearances from the grave, eating with the disciples, or ascension. These constitute significant omissions. Why would Paul, the earliest writer on record, choose to omit these references which were so prominent in the later Gospels?

It must be noted that prior to his vision on the road to Damascus, Paul was a devout Jew whose mission had been to persecute the emerging Christians. In Acts 9:3-9, Paul's vision is described as a "light from heaven..." The passage further states that the men traveling with him "heard the sound but did not see anyone." After this experience, Paul was blind for three days.

It would be less controversial to argue that Paul's vision on the road to Damascus was more subjective than objective. The text says that the men "heard the sound." What sound? Jesus is talking to Paul (Saul). Clearly some problems from the Greek translation are present here.

Let's approach the issue from a different angle. In Corinthians 1:15-17, Paul makes a startling declaration. "But when God, who set me apart from birth and called me by his grace, was pleased to reveal his Son in me so that I may preach him among the Gentiles."

The word "reveal" uses the Greek version of *ophthe*. I'm indebted to Bishop Spong and Robert Funk for describing the various difficulties in translations. I can't do better than quote the good Bishop. "*Ophthe* means to have one's eyes opened to see dimensions beyond the physical. It means to have a revealed encounter with the holy. It relates to the nature of visions, but not so much subjective hallucinations as seeing into that which is ultimately real, into God or God's inbreaking future."[2]

Again, we must keep in mind that Jesus's native tongue was Aramaicc. He must also have spoken Greek.[3] I had never appreciated the range of translation problems until I read Funk's *Honest to Jesus*.[4] The meaning of a word is context driven. To capture the nuances of what is being conveyed, we have to be sensitive to the regular context.

Our perception of reality is influenced through the language we use. Or perhaps, vice versa. We would expect the Eskimos to use many different words to describe "snow" since it is so ubiquitous in their daily life.

Another culture may attach only one meaning to the word since its importance is diminished. Words help us to make sense of reality that we experience in a subjective and cultural sense.

When we go from one translation to another, we should expect something to be lost in the process. It reminds me of rounding-off in mathematics. The particular round-off error may be small, but in the aggregate, the cumulative error may be more significant. That is why I agree with Funk when he writes that every translation is a betrayal.[5] Understand the translation sequence. We are going from Aramaic to Greek to English. Is it reasonable to expect this translation process to fully capture the intended meaning?

Funk writes that the Greek word *kai* usually means "and." However, depending upon the context it can also mean "also, then, at this (that) point, so, next, but, yet, nevertheless, in spite of that, and then, and so, and many similar and related expressions in English."[6]

I was particularly struck by Funk's point concerning the word "leper." Leprosy is a cruel affliction characterized by lesions on the skin including white scaly scabs. It is a very infectious disease, which is why lepers were usually ostracized by society. Its technical name is Hansen's Disease.

In the Greek definition of leprosy, the meaning is broadened to include eczema, psoriasis, skin rash, or any general kind of lesion. The problem that emerges is to properly translate the text to capture the meaning of the experience. To say that someone comes to Jesus with a skin rash and is immediately cured doesn't do justice to the Gospel writers' intentions of depicting Jesus with miraculous power. Hence, the bias will be to interpret the meaning of the term leper or leprosy in the most serious light.

Let's take one more example to make the point. In the Old Testament, Jews were forbidden to articulate God's real name, Jehovah, or in later versions, Yahweh. Over time the phrase Lord God was used as a substitution. As the process evolved, the phrase was shortened to just Lord. The problem with employing the word Lord as a stand-in for God is that there is a range of meanings, from "a master or ruler, a chief, prince, or sovereign, a feudal superior as in "lord of the manor," and it can also be used as a designation for God and title for Jesus."[7]

For Paul, the description "Lord Jesus Christ" is invoked frequently. But Paul wasn't a Trinitarian. For him, Jesus is separate and different from God.

It is particularly interesting that in these earliest, undisputed writings concerning the life of Jesus, the resurrection is viewed as a passive process. That is, Jesus is passive. He is being acted upon by the Father. In Romans 6:9 we read, "Christ being raised from the dead will never die again..." In 1 Thessalonians 1:9 we read, "...and how you turned to God from idols, to serve a living and true God, and to wait for his son from heaven whom he raised from the dead. " In Corinthians 15:4, we note that, "...he was raised on the third day...."

Now if God is doing the raising and Jesus is the passive recipient, how do we reconcile these scriptural texts with Jesus being equal with God?

If Jesus's life stopped here, the picture of Jesus that would emerge would be so utterly different from present day Gospel beleifs . With that caveat in background, let's freeze this snapshot and pull out the separate strands that Paul gave testimony to.

1. With regards to revelatory experiences of the risen Jesus, Paul goes to great length to distinguish the "spiritual body" from the "flesh and blood body." He goes on to say that, "Flesh and Blood cannot inherit the Kingdom of God" (1 Corinthians 15:50). Only the spiritual body can sit at the right hand of God (Colossians 3:1). All of Paul's writings would be consistent with the idea that the Jesus that arose was in spiritual form.

2. What is significant is the omissions which are later present in the Gospels. For example, there is no reference to a virgin birth in any of Paul's writings. In fact, the reference made is that it was a normal birth. According to Paul, "Jesus...was descended from David according to the flesh and designated Son of God in power according to the spiritual holiness by his resurrection from the dead" (Romans 1:3-4). Would it not be reasonable to conclude that a virgin birth would have constituted enough of a miracle to at least include a passing reference in Paul? I find this omission compelling in what it signifies. But more on that later.

3. There are no references to the empty tomb. Again, we must ask ourselves, why is it that Paul omits such an important event which is featured so prominently in later Gospels? I mentioned earlier that the sequence of the writings is critical in evaluating the accretions and embellishments of later writers.

Despite the critical analysis, I find Paul's writings profound and sincere. The resurrection appearances need explaining. The passages in 1 Corinthians 15:3-58 are so revealing. First, I find it interesting that Paul has Jesus appearing first to Cephas or Peter. There is little question that the reason for listing Peter first had to do with establishing the church hierarchy. That is, the appearance of Jesus constitutes powerful expressions of conferring power. Power was conferred in two ways: (1) those who saw Jesus, and (2) those who saw Jesus first. Special status was, of course, given to the disciples. Hence, if one was part of Jesus's inner circle and happened to be first to see Jesus, then power and authority was conferred.

But what I also find dissonant about these appearances is their different manifestations. We have noted that for Paul, the vision blinded him for three days while his companions didn't see the light.

Paul compounds the problem by equating his experience of the risen Jesus to that of the others. As mentioned earlier, the Greek term *ophthe* is used frequently. The clear deduction is that this was a trance experience. A trance experience is by definition subjective. And yet, it is difficult to believe that five hundred people can have such an experience at the same time.

No other Gospel writer mentions the appearance to the five hundred. In fact, no other historian of the time alludes to such as event. We don't know the impact that the risen Jesus had upon the five hundred. But we do know that for the apostles, the resurrection transformed their lives.

I'm always impressed when I hear stories about people being changed. Attitudes and beliefs are difficult to alter. Clearly, something happened to the disciples that they would be willing to die for...

When I am confronted by such an experience, I don't dismiss it lightly. Do we have any precedent in history where people went to their death to preserve a lie? We have heard stories where people have died for a cause whether it be for country, religion, or family. But these are personal encounters. We can't fully define the nature of these experiences. But because words fail us in our attempt at explanation is no reason to cavalierly dismiss such profound experiences.

The personal experiences with the eleven disciples given the absence of Judas are not given a time frame. It is difficult to experience such an event as a mass hallucination since hallucinations are by definition private, i.e., subjective events. Was this a transcedental experience ? And is the problem that our language fails us in describing an encounter with the divine? I wish to return to these questions later.

Before leaving Paul, I would like to make one more comment on the famous Corinthian passage. The syllogism runs as follows:

"If there is no resurrection of the dead, then not even Christ has been raised. And if Christ has not been raised, then our proclamation has been in vain and your faith has been in vain."

Then later in the same paragraph, Paul reverses the sequence. "For if the dead are not raised, then Christ has not been raised either." (1 Corinthians 15:13-16).

I find this to be a very confusing passage. The Pharisees, of which Paul had been a member, believed in the general resurrection at the end of time. A personal resurrection was not allowed within that faith. Later Paul asserts that "...in fact Christ has been raised from the dead, the first fruits of these who have fallen asleep." (1 Corinthians 15:20).

What I find especially significant about this passage is its apocalyptic framework. Jesus was the first to arise. The end of the world was near. That is, God's kingdom would be brought down to earth. Paul went further: God's kingdom had already begun.

The "Kingdom of God is not food and drink but righteousness and peace and joy in the Holy Spirit" (Romans 14:17). We see further evidence that the kingdom of God had begun in Paul's letter to the Thessalonians. Some members of the congregation have died. The survivors are concerned that they didn't have the opportunity to see the Lord return while they were still alive. Paul assures them that the "appearance of the Lord will not precede those who have fallen asleep" (Thessalonians 4:15).

After Jesus's death and resurrection, his followers had taught that the "Son of Man" would return immediately. As the expectations failed to be realized, different explanations had to be offered. With the death of each remaining disciple, the tension mounted. The coming of the kingdom had to be postponed further and further into the future. Finally, Peter offered the ultimate justification. "But do not forget this one thing, dear friends, with the Lord a day is like a thousand years, and a thousand years is like a day" (2 Peter 3:8).

The stage is now set. The seeds of maintaining Christian continuity have been planted. The foundation has been laid. It is only with this background in mind that we can now begin to fully examine the Gospel accounts in chronological order.

Chapter Three: The Gospel of Mark

Approximately 32-37 years have elapsed since the death of Jesus. Again, sometimes it is more instructive to look at what is being omitted. For Mark, there is no mention of: (1) The Virgin Birth, (2) Joseph, the father of Jesus, or (3) Post-resurrection experiences.

In fact, the Markan narrative is so oblivious to time parameters, that we can compress the entire Gospel into four weeks.

Again, let us take this Gospel as a snapshot and freeze it. If we take the writings of Paul and Mark, independent of the other Gospel writers, the image of Jesus that would emerge would be so radically different from the modern-day conception. However, the seeds for the later embellishment have already begun to bear fruit.

Chapter Sixteen of Mark consists of eight verses. Verses 9-20 do not appear in the earliest manuscripts. Mark begins with a quotation from the prophet Isaiah predicting that John the Baptist would pave the way for the coming of the Lord.

As we move through the Markan text, note the attitude of Jesus's family towards Jesus. There are two references in Mark reflecting this attitude. "When his family heard about this, they went to take charge of him, for they said, 'He is out of his mind'" (Mark 3:21).

In a later passage, Jesus was informed that his mother and brothers were waiting for him outside. "Then he looked at those seated in a circle around him and said, "Here are my mother and my brothers! Whoever does God's will is my brother and sister and mother?" (Mark 3:34)

The latter passage may be interpreted to reflect the contrast between those who accept or reject Jesus. Those who had accepted him are his real family.

The previous message is more elusive in its meaning. According to the Quest Study Bible, Jesus's family thought he was crazy because of "His incredible claims, mass popularity, and unusual behavior..."[1]

I find the inconsistency glaring. If we try to reconcile this passage with the later Gospels of Matthew and Luke, the conflict becomes insurmountable. Here we have a miraculous birth, the arrival of the Three Wise Men, the gifts, the star, and the many miracles up to that point in the story. Why should it then surprise Jesus's family that Jesus was not an ordinary man?

I marvel at the skepticism here. Jesus's own mother is skeptical of her son's claims. Perhaps we can account for the brothers' and sisters' incredulity. But Mary's doubts are simply unfathomable.

Furthermore, where is the father in this scene? It should be noted for most of its history, Judea was a deeply rooted patriarchal society. The male was the center of authority and power. Women were not allowed to own property.

The passage in Mark 6:3 is a curious one. "Isn't this the carpenter? Isn't this the son of Mary, the brother of James, Joseph, Judas, and Simon?" In this historical context, it was considered a slur to describe a man's lineage without reference to a father. In no other Old Testament story that I am familiar with is the mother used to describe the lineage.

I believe it is reasonable to raise suspicion as to why Joseph's name was omitted. When facts are missing, speculation soars.

For Bishop Spong, Joseph never existed. Rather, Joseph is a midrashic invention paralleling the Joseph featured in Genesis. I find the similarities striking and persuasive.[2]

The other observation that strikes me when I read Mark is how little respect Jesus seems to have for his own family. As mentioned previously, in this patriarchal society, a woman wasn't permitted the means to sustain her own livelihood. Hence, marriage was the norm.

I suspect that if a sociological study was done of the disciples' families left behind, an enveloping story of resentment and anger would follow. Peter tells Jesus that they (the disciples) have left everything to follow him. Jesus replies that rewards await those who have abandoned their families to follow him.

My first reaction to this recounting of the exemplary life of Jesus would be:: Is this responsible behavior? I think in general, we would condemn any individual who abandons his family to follow a cause. But to leave one's family vulnerable at a subsistence level isn't praiseworthy. The end doesn't justify the means.

The comparison of Jesus in other contexts is strongly contradicted by the abandonment of families which he spawned and encouraged. How do we reconcile these opposing themes?

Rescue comes from unconventional sources. In The Five Gospels, the Jesus Seminar scholars relegated this passage to the black category, i.e., Jesus did not say the passages attributed to him in Mark 10:29-31. Rather, they were edited by his followers to suit the needs of the community.[3]

A: The Triumphal Entry

As a prelude to his entry in Jerusalem, Jesus for the first time in Mark predicts his death. The crucifixion is foretold in Psalm 22:16-18 and Isaiah 53:4-7. I shall make reference to these passages shortly.

But for now, I must ask this question: In the socio-economic contexts of Judea, the oppressed Jews were awaiting a conquering hero. How was the Messiah transformed from a conquering hero as specifically told in Luke 1:32 to the suffering servant?

The so-called triumphant entry into Jerusalem is a fulfillment of Zechariah 9:9, "Your king comes to you...riding a donkey." The context of this passage refers to God's vengeance upon the enemies of Israel. It goes on to say that the king "will take away the chariots from Ephraim and the war worsen from Jerusalem and the battle bow will be broken." Even though the donkey symbolizes humility, this latter passage clearly reveals the image of a warrior.

Even the shouts of the people presage the coming of the warrior-king. "Blessed is the coming kingdom of our father David" (Mark 1:10).

How did Jesus view his role? Or more specifically, did Jesus view himself as the Messiah? "Messiah" meant the anointed one. Its actual usage begins with Paul's letters.

There were three classes of people that were considered anointed: priests, prophets, and kings. As mentioned previously, all references to David engender the category of king. However, as Sanders notes, it is possible to make reference to David as a military leader while God does the fighting.[4]

In general, there are simply too many Davidic references symbolizing a war-rior-king to allow Sanders to muddy the waters. Even if we accept the notion of two messiahs: one warrior–son of David–and the other Priestly–son of Aaron–the meaning still remains the same for the Davidic side.[5]

When Jesus asked the disciples "Who do people say I am?" Peter offered the response, "You are the Christ." Christ admonishes him not to tell anyone. Jesus goes on to refer to himself in a more generic, ambiguous title "Son of Man." But in Mark (15:2) the reference to the King of the Jews is again obvious. Bear in mind that one of the possible meanings of "Christ" was king. Hence, the use of the term "king" is tantamount to "Christ."

If Jesus wished to disavow himself from the use of the little "Messiah" that Sanders implies, then he failed miserably. Occasional ambiguity must not override repeated assertions to the contrary.

We must allow the possibility that Jesus's followers added the designation of Messiah after his death. Within the political climate of Judea, the use of the term "messiah" carried political overtones of liberation. Such a title would clearly come to the attention of the Roman authorities. Perhaps that is why he urged secrecy and used the more neutral term the "Son of Man."

B: The Arrival of the Kingdom

In certain instances, the symbolism becomes compelling. For example, the use of the number twelve is instructive if not provocative. Recall that in Jewish history, there were twelve tribes each descendant of Jacob's twelve sons. Up to the period of 1000 BCE, the tribes were divided into the Northern and Southern kingdoms. The Northern Kingdom consisted of ten tribes while the other two occupied the south. In approximately 800 BCE, the northern tribes were conquered by the Assyrians. To minimize the risk of rebellion, the Assyrians made a typical practice of scattering the populace.

In later years, the Southern Kingdom was conquered by the Babylonians. The Babylonians promoted integration within their culture. Subsequently, the Jewish leaders reestablished the state of "Judah."

The ten lost tribes of Israel were remembered through Jewish history. Aspirations ran high that God would directly intervene to restore Israel's twelve tribes.

I mention this brief excursion in history because Jesus's choosing twelve disciples isn't entirely coincidental.

But when was the kingdom of God to arrive? As I argued in the earlier chapter on Paul, for Jesus it had already come. But this is a controversial point!

In his book *The First Coming*, Thomas Sheehan argues that " the clue to understanding the progressive enhancement of Jesus's status from failed prophet to divine savior lies in the early believers' response to this problem of the interval."[6]

In other words, a Second Coming was expected after Jesus's death. According to Sheehan, the early believers mentioned that the Jesus of the future would appear as "God's apocalyptic deputy."[7] That is, the Jesus of the past had been an eschatological prophet but his future role would be that of the Son of Man.

When Jesus is asked by the high priest if he is the Messiah, he responds, "I am, and you will see the Son of Man at the right hand of the power and coming with the clouds of heaven" (Mark 14:62). Note that when Jesus uses the term "Son of Man" the reference is always to a future individual separate from Jesus.[8]

In either case, if one accepts that Jesus was the Messiah or that Jesus's return was imminent, the dilemma is the same. What happens during this interval if the expectations fail to reach their full flowering?

In the following section, I will continue relying heavily upon Sheehan's work. The Hellenistic Christians became the focal point for the emerging Christology. "Whereas the Aramaic speaking Jews hoped Jesus would become the Messiah at the end of the world, the Hellenistic Jewish converts came to believe that he had already been constituted the Messiah from his mother's womb."[9]

It is interesting to follow the progression of when Jesus became the "Christ." In Mark, it is signified by Jesus's baptism by John. In Matthew and Luke, it is from conception. In John, it is noted from the very beginning of time.

The progression is striking. In addition, as the Gospel tradition develops, I will show that Jesus becomes a more active agent especially as it relates to the resurrection.

Sheehan lists the stages that the early church passed through in depicting Jesus as the Suffering Servant. In the first stage, his disciples gave new meaning to Jesus's death as a "martyred prophet who had been rejected by men but glorified by God."[10]

The second stage occurred when the crucifixion was recast into an "eschatological inevitability." That is, Jesus's suffering was not in vain but the fulfillment of God's plan.

It is at the final stage that the circle is completed. "...Perhaps before mid-century - did Hellenistic Jewish Christians begin to think of Jesus's death as a vicarious atonement for the sins of mankind."[11]

The resurrection was elevated to assume transcendent meaning. The focus shifted from an "apocalyptic future to a heavenly present."[12] It was no longer important nor even relevant to expect Jesus's return. The present moment had become impregnated with religious meaning. Jesus had died for our sins. His atonement was complete. The sacrifice of the paschal lamb was no longer needed. As mentioned previously, I think that it is plausible to conclude that Jesus's remarks can be construed to mean that the "Son of Man" would come in the near future. But then the prediction is falsified. Jesus is crucified! Hence, it is difficult to elevate the status of a prophet whose fundamental prediction failed to materialize.

I'm struck by the stark contradictions in the weave of this fabric. If Jesus's purpose was to become the Suffering Servant in Isaiah, then why that painful and distressful interlude in the Garden of Gethsemane? "My soul is overwhelmed with sorrow to the point of death" (Matthew 26:36).

Death was the dramatic conclusion to Jesus's mission. It was to be expected. It had even been ordained by God. All events had to converge upon Jesus's death to fulfill the Scriptures or more specifically, Isaiah. But why the doubts, fear, and angst? And why the cry on the cross? "My God, my God, why have you forsaken me" (Matthew 27:46, Mark 15:34).

Furthermore, does it not make a mockery of the meaning of sacrifice to know that your death is illusory? That is, within three days you will arise and take your rightful place in the kingdom of God.

It is at junctures like these that literal interpretations break apart through the force of inconsistencies. Only the use of Midrash can bring harmony into this web.

To properly understand the concept of the Suffering Servant, we must go back and appreciate the Jewish context of sacrifice. In the religious tradition, the Jews believed in a concept called the treasury of merit. The chief accountant was the Lord himself. The idea was that each individual had something akin to a ledger account. From time to time, the Lord would intervene to balance the scales.[13]

Within this context, the belief was that each individual was responsible for his own actions and to some extent bore responsibility for the nation. Hence, individual and collective responsibility was interwoven.

The use of sacrifice—i.e., slaughtering of animals—was a way to balance the scales for the many. If an individual had an excess of virtue, then through sacrifice he could engender some virtue to help balance the scales for others. In general, the more unblemished the sacrificial animal, the greater amount of virtue to be reaped.

The story of Abraham offering his son Isaac was understood midrashically adumbrating the story of Jesus as the perfect sacrifice. Just as a sacrificial animal could partially atone for our sins, then the perfect sacrifice embodied in Jesus would become the ultimate redemption. "So Jews who acknowledged Jesus as Lord had no further need for sacrifices. They had no further need for atonement, Jesus had made the perfect sacrifice, he offered himself."[14]

When Paul wrote that Christ had died according to Scripture the obvious and only reference was to Isaiah. I say "only" because a fair conclusion would be that the majority of references referred to the coming of a warrior-king. The concept of a "Suffering Servant" was an interesting twist and was consistent within the Jewish context of sacrifice. In Isaiah 52 and 53, we now have the basis for a new and different midrashic interpretation of Jesus.

But even this interpretation presents difficulties. First, Jesus, by his own admission, came to "Fulfill the Law or the Prophets." If you would ask a Hindu or Buddhist what this means, you would be greeted with complete bemusement. The point is that this statement only makes sense within the context of the Old Testament. The Old Testament has meaning only in the context of Jewish history. Is it not unusual for an omnipotent and all-loving God to provide redemption for only part of his people. I find the use of these human frailties projected upon God as pure anthropomorphism.

Furthermore, examine the earlier Jewish context of sacrifice. How does the sacrifice of one's son bring about redemption? If a sacrifice is to be weighed by a degree of value, then on that theory killing one's spouse, son, or daughter should have greater redemptive value. And what kind of father would demand the death of his son to atone for the sins of the world? This kind of collective guilt is on par with holding the entire German nation for the atrocities of the Nazis. Is it reasonable to hold a family, let alone a nation, responsible for the transgressions of a few members? Would we not deplore this if it was asked of us individually? And yet when placed within a religious context, we marvel at God's compassion. And how is Jesus equal with God? If one believes in the concept of the Holy Trinity, then paradoxically, doesn't this mean that God is sacrificing himself? How does this have any meaning beyond blind faith?

I find nothing compassionate about an omniscient God who allows the inevitable to occur and finds fault accordingly. But more on this later on in my chapter on God.

My point is that very few people bother to ask these kinds of legitimate questions. I agree with Bishop Spong's claim that when we literalize these midrashic stories, they die from the weight of their internal contradictions. These stories point the way to a literalness that must be transcended if we are to embrace their religious meaning.

Chapter Four: The Gospel of Luke

The Christian tradition was growing rapidly in the 80s CE. The polarization between the Jewish Christians and other orthodox Jews was widening. The Romans had just completed the destruction of Jerusalem. Political and social tension was growing. People were being asked to take sides.

During the time of crisis, it is common for people to revert to the anchors of their faith. For the Jewish people, one such anchor had always been the Torah. Hence, we see a turn to more literal and traditional adherence to the Torah.

Jewish Christians rejected this forced fundamentalism. Didn't Jesus dine with all kinds of people from beggars, tax collectors, fishermen, etc? Hence, wouldn't the Jewish laws of kosher go against the Jewish teaching of an open food table?

In addition, the Christian day of resurrection (Sunday) had begun to compete against the Jewish Sabbath (Saturday).

As the battle lines were being drawn, the present-day image of Jesus began to emerge. The emergence of several new themes began to form. Apparently, fifty years had passed since the death of Jesus. At this juncture, we have no virgin birth stories and no mentioning of direct accounts of post-resurrection experiences.

I want to tackle these omissions and try to understand the social context that gave rise to their occurrence. As mentioned earlier in Mark, the holy spirit had entered Jesus at the time of baptism by John. However, there is a problem if this scenario is allowed to stand.

In a deeply patriarchal society, we have no reference to Jesus's father. Rumors had begun to emerge alleging that Jesus was born illegitimately.

Furthermore, the attempt was made to portray Jesus as greater than John the Baptist. The fact that Jesus had been baptized by John was an embarrassing detail that was preserved by the force of truthfulness. That was subversive enough!

John had been shown to be a post-menopausal birth. How does one make Jesus the greater figure and lay to rest the circulating rumors? The solution to this puzzle rests in the virgin birth idea.

The virgin birth conception didn't originate with Christianity. Gautama–the Buddha–Zoroaster (600 BCE), and Krishna (1200 BCE) are just a few historic figures whose birth was attributed to a virgin mother.

Note further that Luke–who many believe wrote before Matthew–was a Gentile. We also know that Luke was more familiar with Greek than Hebrew. How? Because the Greek translation of the Scriptures known as the Septuagint was used exclusively by Luke to quote from the Scriptures. These Scriptures had been translated into Greek between 250 and 130 BCE.

The sequence is critical. I believe that Luke, being less familiar with Hebrew practices and tradition, was more likely to engage in an error of Hebrew translation.

In Isaiah 7:14, the Hebrew word *almah* means "young woman." Luke, being more familiar with Greek than Hebrew, interpreted *almah* as the Greek equivalent of *parthenos*. In Greek, *parthenos* means "virgin." But that is not what the Hebrew text intended. If the translation was rendered "virgin," then there was a specific Hebrew word intended for that use: *betulah*.

I find it compelling that the word *betulah* is used fifty times in the Hebrew Scriptures with the same meaning. Alternately, the word "almah" is used nine times, and nowhere does it mean "virgin".[1]

It is curious that John, who came later than Luke and Matthew, makes no mention of virgin birth.

I also find it amusing that after Luke goes to great lengths to establish the virginity of Mary, he proceeds to trace Jesus's genealogy through Joseph. But doen't the idea of a virgin birth establish a genealogy independent of the father?

Further, it should be noted in a pre-Mendelian society there was no under-standing of a male's sperm fertilizing the female's egg. The woman was thought to contribute nothing to the birth of a baby. Within that limited context, there is no concern with the implication of violating biological laws.

I would also add that in an age without television, radio, and newspapers, and where 90% of the population is illiterate, how does Luke know Jesus's gene-alogy? I won't dwell on the incompatibility with Matthew's genealogy, but I have never heard anyone try to account for the accuracy of Luke's and Matthew's ge-nealogies. In an era of limited records and varying cultures, how realistic are these documents?

One final footnote: I find it compelling that no less an authority than Ray-mond E. Brown–one of the great Catholic theologians–admits that there is no ev-idence that they–OT writers–"foresaw with precision over a single detail in the life of Jesus of Nazareth."

Brown adds an interesting insight. The presence of the definite article "the" to "young girl" indicated that Isaiah was referring to the identity of someone that was known to him. And Brown concludes, "... Isaiah 7:14 does not refer to a virginal conception in the distant future. The sign offered by the prophet was the immi-nent birth of a child, probably Davidic, but naturally conceived, who would illus-trate God's providential care for his people."[2]

Furthermore, I've often wondered if anyone ever looks at the context of these reported prophecies. The historical background is the Syro-Ephraimite war in the early part of the eighth century BCE. Israel is divided between the Northern King-dom controlled by Assyria while the Southern Kingdom is relatively autonomous. The Assyrians are on the move while King Ahaz sits on the throne in Jerusalem.

The Assyrian threat forces the temporary alliance between King Pekah of Is-rael based out of Samaria and King Rezin of Syria based in Damascus. Despite the alliance, both Pekah and Rezin fear that they are still outnumbered. Hence, they approach King Ahaz of Jerusalem to strengthen their alliance.

Ahaz is emboldened by his emissary Isaiah to stand firm and predicts that within a generation both Pekah and Rezin will be destroyed. Ahaz refuses to join the alliance. Both Pekah and Rezin become angered. They proceed to mobilize their forces around Jerusalem. Their intention is to defeat Ahaz and place a more cooperative king on the throne. Jerusalem becomes a sieged city.

Ahaz tells Isaiah to ask the Lord for a sign to prove the accuracy of the prophecy that Pekah and Rezin would be destroyed. Isaiah replies that he "will not put God to the test."

Ahaz is angered at Isaiah's response. Hence, he proceeds to give the answer that Ahaz refused to hear. "Therefore the Lord himself will give you a sign: the virgin will be with child and will give birth to a son and will call him Immanuel" (Isaiah 7:14).

Again I pose the question: Is this really foretelling the arrival of Jesus by several hundreds of years? The passage makes reference that he will "eat curds and honey when he knows how to refuse the evil and choose the good" (Isaiah 7:15). Upon reaching this point when he can distinguish right from wrong. "The land of the two kings you dread will be laid waste" (Isaiah 7:16).

This is the context for Isaiah's prophecy of Jesus's virgin birth. Upon Israel paying off its debt to the Lord in the form of being taken captive by Babylon, God would come to the rescue.

If one reads Isaiah 40, there is reference to a Sovereign Lord that comes with power. But I fail to see how the coming of Jesus signaled the liberation of a suppressed people. The passage makes clear that these events would happen within a span of seventeen years and not seven hundred years later. Furthermore, the symbolism, as we shall see in later Gospels, is one of a conquering Messiah descended from the House of David. In my reading of Isaiah 7, a few lines have been misappropriated to satisfy preconceived suppositions. If one studies carefully the context, this is indeed prophecy historicized. That is, an Old Testament passage has been stretched to accord with Old Testament prophecy.

A: Resurrection in Luke

In the rest of this chapter, I wish to examine the resurrection in Luke. Before I turn to that task, I wish to note a few observations that strike me as odd and in need of further explanation.

First, what is Judas betraying? Jesus preached daily in the temple. His appearance was well known as evidenced by his entry into Jerusalem. My reading of Luke indicates that the Mount of Olives (Garden of Gethsemane) was a regular meeting place. What precisely was the action that constituted betrayal?

What was Jesus's crime? Surely, it wasn't because he was the Messiah. Jesus lived in a messianic age of prophets and would-be kings. Many people claimed to be the messiah without repercussions from the Sanhedrin. The claims to "Messiah" or "Son of God" didn't by themselves constitute blasphemy.[3]

According to Sanders, Caiaphas was the mediator between the Jewish people and the Roman officials. "...He did not act because of theological disagreement, but because of his principal, political and moral responsibility: to preserve the peace and prevent riots and bloodshed."[4]

Another perspective advanced by Sheehan states that Jesus was "defying the authority of the religious establishment."[5] We must remember that Jesus's Christology usurped religious authority. The temple had been the center of religious worship. In effect, it constituted the mediating link between heaven and earth. Or God and his children. Jesus claims that the kingdom of God was "within" meant in part that the relationship between God and man could be established directly without any intermediaries. Both explanations are equally plausible.

Secondly, the meeting before the Sanhedrin, as described by Luke reads like an eyewitness account. Upon the arrest of Jesus, the disciple "forsook him and fled." Where does the recorded text before the Sanhedrin come from?

Luke has taken Jesus to the high priest that same night following his arrest. Upon morning, the Sanhedrin convened. This is a much more likely scenario than what occurred in Matthew where the Sanhedrin meets during the same night as Jesus's arrest–an obvious transgression of the Torah.

Pertaining to the Resurrection, Luke has the women (Mary Magdalene, Joanna, Mary the Mother of Jesus, and others) visiting the tomb the first day of the week. As I read this account, the thing that struck me as really odd was the women's motive. In John, we read that seventy-five pounds of myrrh and aloes were used to wrap Jesus's body. The entire purpose for sealing the tomb was to prevent tampering with Jesus's body. And yet, my analysis of Luke is that the women were expecting the stone to be rolled back by either the Roman guard or the temple soldiers. But why? Where did this explanation come from?

I understand the paradoxical claim that having the women witness the empty tomb heightened the veracity of the reported event. The justification is that if this event was contrived, the author wouldn't have chosen the women as witnesses.

The entire event seems contrived. What must be remembered was that Jesus was convicted and crucified as a criminal. Crucifixion was the most severe penalty that could be imposed upon any individual.

We must separate history from faith if we are going to do justice to the story. How likely would it have been that Joseph, a member of the Council, would come forth after Jesus's death to offer a lavish burial after his own peers had voted to condemn him? Such action would certainly bring sharp rebuke and criticism from the members of the Sanhedrin. If we follow the historical line, it is difficult to believe that a lowly peasant would merit such a reward after a public, horrific execution.

In addition, the release of Barabbas is difficult to believe. Pontius Pilate is made to serve the dictates of the people. The people demand that Jesus be crucified and that Barabbas be released. There is no independent extra-biblical source that confirms this custom of releasing a prisoner during Passover.

Barabbas was an admitted revolutionary and enemy of Rome. It is doubtful that in this unstable political climate that the Romans would aggravate their vulnerability by releasing such a dangerous prisoner.

The image of Pilate before the people is out of character. We have two accounts by non-Christian sources that speak of a brutal tyrant. In the Antiquities 18:56, Josephus describes the episode when Pilate became the procurator of Judea. Jewish practices forbade the use of embossed medallions of the emperor. Not wishing to antagonize the Jewish subjects, previous procurators "used standards that had no such ornament. Pilate was the first to bring the images into Jerusalem and set them up, doing it without the knowledge of the people, for he entered at night."[6]

After the people vehemently protested, the whole city went on a collective sit-down strike. Pilate summoned the demonstrators before his court. He threatened to kill all of them unless the strike ended. To Pilate's surprise, they were all willing to accept martyrdom than betray the precepts of their faith. Facing a total massacre and a potential revolt, Pilate reluctantly agreed to their demands.

The second incident involved the use of temple funds to finance the construction of an aqueduct. When the Sanhedrin protested, Pilate intermingled his troops in civilian dress with the crowd. Pilate gave the orders "not to use their swords, but to beat any rioters with cudgels."[7]

Both incidents reveal Pilate to be provocative and ready to use force when the situation demanded. It is difficult to reconcile this historical image of Pilate with that contained in the Gospels.

It is curious that Pilate becomes more noble, i.e., less willing to crucify Jesus as the Gospels evolved. For example, in Mark 15:9 we have Pilate "knowing it was out of envy that the chief priests had handed Jesus over to him." Pilate is portrayed as the passive judge ready to be swayed by the collective judgment of the crowd. In Mark 15:15 we read that "Wanting to satisfy the crowd, Pilate released Barabbas to them." By the time we get to John–the last Gospel written–Pilate is even more resistive and reluctant to crucify Jesus.

Before we move on, allow me a few more observations about these passages. The historical context in which Jesus lived was an age of repression and subversion. A conquered people usually despise the rulers. The Jewish people were no exception.

The Jews were a proud culture. Within the collective psyche burned the torch of freedom leading to the restoration of the Davidic throne. In short, the Jewish nation constituted a tinderbox of rage and repression ready to explode under the guise of an effective leader.

Jesus's actions were highly provocative. His turning of the money tables, his triumphal entry, his notion that the kingdom of God was within, etc. are themes which were subversive to the social order.

"Envy" is hardly the right word to describe the motivation of the Jewish leaders. In addition, I would ask: envious of what? We need to remind ourselves that Jesus and the members of the Sanhedrin were all Jews. If Jesus was the fulfillment of prophecy, why was he not embraced accordingly?

Imagine this scenario. Your people have been waiting for a thousand years for a new King David to emerge. You know that the prophet Zechariah had predicted that a king riding a donkey would enter Jerusalem. According to the Gospel writers, Jesus enters Jerusalem precisely as predicted. The huge crowds that waited along the way to greet him could only assure that his presence became known to the Jewish and Roman authorities.

Furthermore, you've been told that this Jesus is a miracle worker who performs wondrous feats. Question: given this set of premises, would it not make sense to gather more information about this individual's identity? It makes little sense to arrest the individual and force him to appear before you. Rather you ask the person to give you some sign to confirm his true identity...

One more point. I find it very curious that the crowd would choose Barabbas over Jesus for release. From the Gospel accounts, we read how the people lined Jesus's path with leaves, palm branches, and even garments upon his entry into Jerusalem. Why would the people betray his popularity several days later? We know that Barabbas was according to Luke a murderer and rebel (Luke 23:19). In Matthew's account, we have chief priests persuading the crowd to favor Barabbas over Jesus. If the Jewish rulers' objective was to preserve the social order, I fail to see how releasing a revolutionary would facilitate that end.

Literal interpretations engender contradictions. If one avenue of understanding proves elusive, let us follow a different path. What if the path towards understanding is labeled midrash? Would that trajectory yield any fruit?

John Dominic Crossan notes that in the Barabbas narrative, we have symbolic dramatization of the people choosing "an armed rebel over an unarmed savior."[8] Note that Mark was writing in the late sixties CE. The fall of Jerusalem occurred in 70 AD.

A gradual shift is occurring, crystallized most clearly by Matthew that shifts the blame for the crucifixion of Jesus from Pilate to the Jews (Matthew 27:24-26). The story of Barabbas may simply be a "rhetorical antithesis between the good Jesus and the fictitious bad one so that Jews could be shown for evermore to have rejected his authentic good counterpart."[9]

It is interesting to note that Barabbas literally means "son of the Father" (bar-son, Abba-father, or God). In effect, Jesus was labeled as a fake Messiah and Barabbas (children of God = Jews) was released from bondage.

For me, the meaning of this symbolism was that God would keep his promise to release his chosen people from bondage. But that would happen sometime in the future- independent of Jesus.

B: Shifting the Blame

The culmination of the Roman-Jewish conflict ended with the fall of the Jerusalem temple and all its associated traditions. The temple had for centuries marked the center of Jewish life. Its destruction went well beyond the physical domain. Jewish activity was dominated by the temple as the centerpiece of daily life. The eight Jewish holidays of: Passover, Pentecost, Ninth of Ab, Rosh Hashanah, Atonement, Tabernacles, Dedication, and Purim—revolved around the orbit of the temple.

The Jewish nation was now adrift. It was the customs and traditions practiced for hundreds of years that preserved their identity. At the core, stood the temple. The destruction of the temple was akin to an implosion whose devastation was more significant to the Jewish identity than what the Roman tyranny could ever wreak.

On the other side stood the victorious Romans. The price of victory was steep. The Jewish nation had come to represent an anathema to Roman leaders and citizens. Being Jewish was at a historical ebb within Roman society.

Within this context, conflicting forces are at work. The Jewish culture itself is a house divided. On one end, we find a rigid Jewish orthodoxy. On the other extreme, we find the Hellenized Christians who became converts of Jesus. In the middle, we find a multitude of sects.

The polarization between the two extremes grew. Within time, the Christians became increasingly divorced from their Jewish roots. I believe that it is this latter political fact that most accounts for the rapid proliferation of Christianity. Why is this so?

From a political perspective, the war against the Jews had been costly. It doesn't serve the self-interest of any governor to engage in an internecine battle. The successful governors were those that preserved the peace and paid their bounty to Rome.

We must also recognize that the Jewish faith contained splintered fractures. After the fall of Jerusalem, these sects proceed along different paths. It is not my purpose here to give a detailed description of the various sects. Rather it is to realize that Judaism wasn't homogeneous in the beginning. As the internal divisions grew, its splintering into various sects became inevitable.

A first reading of Acts 8:1-3 suggests that the Christian Church in Jerusalem was persecuted. Stephen—a Hellenized Christian—was stoned to death for violating religious law. Stephen claimed that true worship didn't need to be mediated through temple rites. The stoning of Stephen represented a precursor to the mounting tension between both sides.

One of the most controversial opinions espoused by the Hellenists was that the end of time(eschatology) had dawned with Jesus's death and resurrection. In this new era, temple worship was obviated. This was the main theme of Stephen's speech and the reason why he was executed.

As Christians, both the Hellenized and Jewish sects deviated from traditional Judaism. However, the Hellenized Jews contained the more radical strain. The Hellenists were led by such deacons as Philip and Stephen. The Jewish Christians were led by the apostles.

It is arguable if Christianity could've ever developed without the indefatigable efforts of Paul. In Luke, we see Paul positioned as a Christian removed from the Jewish mainstream. Paul's portrayal was embellished to depict him as being a loyal citizen whose activities constituted no threat to Roman Society.

And what about the underlying theme of Sermons in Acts? According to Burton Mack, "The massage is, "He was your God's choice: you killed him; therefore repent and be baptized, that is, become Christians."[10] In essence, the message constituted intimidation by guilt. That is why more than half of Luke's story centers around the Jewish-Christian conflict.

I mentioned earlier that Roman prejudice against traditional Judaism ran high. In order to succeed, Christianity had to distance itself from its roots. Luke's portrayal of Christianity is that it was "good for the Roman order and thus worthy of Roman support."[11]

The strategy worked beyond all expectations. In an age of repression and injustice, the Jewish concern for a personal God to oversee social justice was most appealing. The destruction of the temple was now recast in a new light with the resurrection marking the starting point for the new movement.

C: The Ascension

Luke is the only Gospel writer to mention the Ascension. He is also the only writer to report Jesus's presence for forty days after the resurrection in Acts assuming common attribution. A few comments on each event are in order.

First, the common understanding of the heavens in the first century AD was that of a dome or canopy. God was believed to dwell just above the sky. The idea that we live on a tiny planet in the midst of an enveloping, infinite blackness was simply unthinkable. Only a first-century mind with their limited view of the universe could imagine Jesus rising to the heavens.

Secondly, while Jesus spends only a few hours in Luke with his disciples, his duration is lengthened to forty days in Acts. I find it astounding that during this lengthy period on earth, only the apostles are the benefactors of his glorious presence. If only his teachings admitted a more encompassing non-Gentile audience, the belief in Jesus would've silenced speculation and strengthened the faith. Why he chose to reveal himself only to his disciples needlessly adds to the continuing mystery. But I think it is legitimate to question this aspect of Luke's Gospel.

In my estimation, it isn't convincing to the non-believer to limit Jesus's resurrection appearances to his disciples only. In all four Gospels, the list of characters includes the two Marys, eleven apostles, and Paul. Only in I Corinthians 15 does the mentioning of appearing to five hundred occur. Paul's language that he "appeared to more than five hundred of the brethren at the same time" suggests that they were also believers.

But why did Jesus choose to appear to believers only? Surely, the fall from grace from the time of Adam afflicted all human beings. Then surely, redemption should apply to all.

One footnote to Luke: The road to Emmaus features the risen Christ walking with Cleopas and a companion. While speculation has continued on the identity of Cleopas mentioned nowhere else in the Bible, one of the characteristics of a spiritual body is that it renders Jesus unrecognizable. I find it curious that in all other respects the person is indistinguishable from any normal human being. But this mark of being unrecognizable isn't permanent. Apparently, at a certain point, the curtain is lifted and his true identity is revealed. What a curious anomaly? No halos, no luminescence. In a word, only, unrecognizability.

But the more important point has to do with how Luke changes the resurrection language from a passive to an active form. That is, up to this juncture, Jesus is merely the recipient of God's actions. Jesus now is pictured as initiating the process. Jesus is no longer raised by God. Jesus raises himself from the grave. The change is significant. For in this evolutionary progression, Jesus will be transformed into God's equal. The Father = The Son = The Holy Spirit. Three faces but one God.

Chapter Five: The Gospel of Matthew

Despite the uncertainty of the authorship, the writer appears to be a Jewish Christian. The time is early to middle eighties CE. The Jews have been utterly defeated at the hands of the Roman legions. The "wailing wall" was the only remnant of the great temple in Jerusalem. The Jews became more despised as their integration into a Greek speaking world quickened.

As a Jewish Christian, Matthew emphasized the Hebrew context to Jesus's life. In fact, in his statement he traces the genealogy of Jesus to "The son of David, the son of Abraham" (Matthew 1:1). Such references clearly show Matthew's Jewish past. As mentioned earlier, over ninety percent of Matthew is contained in Mark. That Matthew relied on Mark is indubitable. Furthermore, as a Jewish scribe, Matthew invoked the sacred writings of the Torah to explain and embellish the life of Jesus.

The historical parallels are too great to dismiss Matthew's accounts as mere coincidence. The slaughter of the innocent by King Herod parallels the tale of Moses's escape from the pharaoh's decree. Where Moses is tested for forty years in the wilderness, Jesus's temptation lasts forty days. Moses emerges from the mountaintop to give his people the Ten Commandments. Likewise, Jesus goes up the mountainside to teach the Beatitudes in the Sermon on the Mount.

Are these parallels merely coincidental, or are they the product of midrashic interpretation? In addition to copying from Mark, we also know that Matthew made constant reference to the OT. How do we know this? For Matthew, Jesus's life and death are the fulfillment of the prophecy. The virgin status of Mary was fulfilled in Isaiah 7:14. The destruction of the children by Herod fulfilled Jeremiah 31:15. Jesus's birthplace was a fulfillment in Micah 5:2. The temptations of Jesus reflect Deuteronomy 6:16, 8:3.

Matthew, in general, is quite explicit in quoting the scripture. The power of midrashic interpretation is prominently thematic. More than any other writer, Matthew treats the Jewish law as authentic and goes to great length to place words in Jesus's mouth to accommodate this basic premise.

Again I ask, are these examples of prophecy being fulfilled or prophecy historicized? The former is a metaphysical explanation. The latter is empirical. What would need to happen to invoke and believe in a metaphysical explanation? Let's take the virgin birth as an example of fulfilled prophecy.

First of all, the context in Isaiah is stretched beyond all recognition. There is no reference in the story to a Messiah who would appear through a virgin birth tradition. Secondly, retrospective analysis to fulfill prophecy has the advantage of hindsight. That is why these legendary accretions develop after the individual's death. Thirdly, we have seen that there are plausible explanations in accounting for different translations. Fourth, I find it remarkable that this tradition is mentioned by only two of the Gospel writers. This omission is most conspicuous. And lastly, I find the mentioning of the virgin birth tradition paralleling the increasing Hellenization of Jewish society.

The Greeks divided the body at about the diaphragm. Below the diaphragm, the body was viewed as lustful, sinful, and material. The nobler passions lay in the mind. I could certainly understand that given this Greek context, the Jesus tradition became embellished to represent Jesus as conquering the flesh as well as death.

It is astonishing to witness how the Jewish context of the life of Jesus is ignored. In Jewish society, it was highly unusual for a Jewish male to be unmarried. In fact, the name "rabbi" used to reference Jesus in several passages presupposes a married male. An unmarried rabbi is an oxymoron. Hence, in this context, the greater explanation would demand why Jesus remained unmarried—not the reverse.

The NT is, of course, silent on this question. And an argument from silence can never be conclusive. But it should make us suspicious of ulterior motives at work.

A: Jesus Sends Out the Twelve

If Jesus was indeed the Messiah, is it not reasonable for him to save all of God's people? Is a Gentile or a Samaritan any less a child of God? I find the exclusivity stifling. Jesus tells his disciples to preach the message to the "lost sheep of Israel" (Matthew 10:6). A God that plays favorites is frightening. Think about the implications of this passage. An all-powerful God sends his only begotten son to cleanse man from original sin. However, the rescue is to be limited to the Jewish people only.

How is a Gentile or some other non-Jewish person to be saved? By accepting Jesus as his Lord and Savior, you reply. But by his own words, he came to save the nation of Israel. What possible purpose would such a savior have for other religions?

According to the Jesus Seminar, this passage is marked by a black designation (i.e., not attributable to Jesus). The consensus of the Fellows of the Seminar was that Jesus's mission had extensive contact with gentiles. Hence, this passage in Matthew is overly restrictive."[1]

B: The Resurrection in Matthew

I'm puzzled by how Matthew as a Jewish scribe repeatedly violates Jewish law in his writings. The meeting before the Sanhedrin on the holy day of Passover was specifically forbidden by the Torah. The Torah was explicit that judgment was to be rendered during the light of day.

I'm bewildered by how frequently Matthew quotes Jesus as saying that his arrest and execution were destined to be a fulfillment of scripture. "Do you think that I cannot call on my Father, and he will at once put at my disposal more than twelve legions of angels? But how then would the Scriptures be fulfilled that say it must happen in this way?" (Matthew 26:53-54)

If Jesus anticipated the events that were to follow, the painful agonizing in the Garden of Gethsemane seems an apparent contradiction.

Furthermore, Jesus cries out on the cross, "My God, my God, why have you forsaken me?" (Matthew 27:45) Again, I find this passage contradictory. In repeated passages in Matthew, we have Jesus describing his arrest, execution, and death as the fulfillment of prophecy. These statements give the appearance that the events were not going according to plan.

Then in an incredible passage, Matthew writes, "At that moment the curtain of the temple was torn in two from top to bottom. The earth shook and the rocks split. The tombs broke open and the bodies of many holy people who had died were raised to life. They came out of the tombs, and after Jesus's resurrection they went into the holy city and appeared to many people" (Matthew 27:51-52).

I find this passage breathtaking! No other Gospel writer mentions this incident. A literal interpretation presents more problems than it solves.

One possible explanation is that the curtain separated the Holy Place from the most Holy of Places. It was in the inner room where God was thought to reside. One interpretation that would be fully consistent with the symbolism of a torn curtain was that the barrier separating man from God was no longer present. An individual could have access to God directly without any intermediaries.

The incident involving the raising of the dead is more problematic. As I mentioned earlier, Jews believed in a general resurrection at the end of time. Wouldn't such a fantastic event be worthy of cursory reference in non-Christian sources?

C: The Guards at the Tomb

Matthew is the only writer that makes reference to Jesus's prediction that he would rise again after three days. Hence, to protect against the possibility of the disciples stealing his body, the chief priests and the Pharisees convinced Pilate to make "the tomb secure by putting a seal on the stone and posting the guard" (Matthew 27:66).

Incidentally, from the time Jesus was buried to his resurrection wasn't three days. If we accept that Jesus was buried just before dusk—approximately 6pm—on Friday and that he arose from the tomb sometime before dawn on Sunday, then we have to conclude that one day and two nights equate to thirty-six hours.

The phrase three days or what later was referred to on the third day had meaning beyond its literal description. In Matthew, we find three examples of righteousness (6:1-18), three prohibitions (6:19,7:6), three injunctions (7:7-20), three healing together (8:1-15), three miracles demonstrating the authority of Jesus (8:23, 9:8), three restorations (9:18-34), three fear-nots (10:26, 28, 31), three types of person unworthy of Jesus (10:37-38), three sayings about "little ones" (18:6, 10, 14), three parables on sowing (13:1-22), three prophetic parables (21:28-22:14), three questions in the passion narrative (22:15-40), three prayers in Gethsemane (26:36-46), three denials of Peter (26:57-75), and three questions of Pilate (27:15-26).

Is this all coincidental? To this list I could also add the concept of the Trinity. Clearly, the number three had some special significance.

In addition, if the tomb was to be sealed for three days, then the women–Mary Magdalene and the other Mary–going to the tomb on that first day of the week would be even more problematic.

The "young man dressed in a white robe" in Mark is now transformed into an angel with "clothes as white as snow."

The angel admonishes the women to go to Galilee to meet the risen Jesus.

The guards became like dead men when the angel of the Lord rolled back the stone. However, the guards still appear conscious during this episode. They report to the chief priest all they had observed.

In Galilee, eleven disciples see the risen Jesus. The text says that some worshipped him while others doubted him (Matthew 28:16-18). Jesus then commissions his eleven disciples to preach the word of God to all nations.

One footnote to this chapter. Among the Gospel writers, Matthew invokes midrashic explanations more than any other. Let us look at the OT stories and see how much of Jesus's resurrection can be accounted for by midrashic interpretation. From Joshua 10:16-18, we have Joshua "roll large rocks up to the mouth of the cave and post some men there to guard it."

From Zachariah, we have "the one they have buried" (12:10) and the scattering of the disciples (13:7).

From Psalm 22 we have "My God, my God, why have you forsaken me? (22:1) and, "Even my bosom friend in whom I trusted, who ate of my bread, has lifted his heel against me" (41:9).

All the elements are now in place to piece together the experience of the resurrection. But much more on the resurrection experience after the chapter on John.

Chapter Six: The Gospel of John

We are now at the turn of the first century, some sixty-seven years after the death of Jesus. I wish to highlight several discrepancies from the synoptic Gospels.

In the synoptic Gospels, Jesus comes to Jerusalem during the climax of his life. In John, Jesus is involved in three Passover celebrations suggesting a tripling of his public ministry. The image of Jesus as the Lamb of God is demonstrated from the time that John first saw Jesus. The uncertainty that John had expressed in prison concerning Jesus's status is now gone. Events depicting Jesus as the Christ emerge very early on.

Compare the Calling of the First Disciples between Mark and John. Again, the entire theme is to more quickly depict Jesus as the Christ.

More than any other Gospel, John employs a symbolism that argues strongly against literalism. Let me cite just a few to caution us against literal interpretations.

> 1. "Destroy this temple and I will raise it again in three days" (2:19).
> 2. "I will tell you the truth, no one can see the Kingdom of God unless he is born again" (3:3).
> 3. "If you know the gift of God and who it is that asks you for a drink, you would have asked him and he would have given you living water" (4:10).

In addition, some of the passages appear to be intermixed with post-Easter sayings. For example, how would a first-century Jew explain these words: "I am the resurrection and the life" (11:25). As I've mentioned previously, a personal resurrection was not part of the Jewish beliefs...

Of all the Gospel writers, John is the most extreme in his use of poetic license. A literal reading can only obfuscate the hidden meaning of a profound experience.

The evolution of Jesus's divinity is now heightened. Jesus is identified with God from the beginning of time. Accordingly, his mission is more definitive. The references to the Davidic throne are now absent. The prophecies of Isaiah are now given prominence,

In the first chapter, John quotes John the Baptist referring to Jesus as the Lamb of God, who takes away the sins of the world. Contrast this development with the other Gospels. In Mark, that linkage is made as late as 8:31. "He then begins to teach them that the Son of Man must suffer many things..."

In Matthew the references to Jesus didn't fit the Davidic model. In Chapter 11, we have John doubting the identity of Jesus.

In Luke, we still see references to Jesus as the son of David (20:41-44, 21:27-28). The political linkage of Jesus to David is strong. The implications are obvious.

But Jesus's mission wasn't that of a conquering hero. Hence, a new paradigm had to be invoked. Enter Isaiah's conception of the Suffering Servant. This became the dominant model to explain the life of Jesus.

I am struck by how compelling and frequent the references to Jesus as the Paschal lamb. Let me cite a few. "Look, the Lamb of God" (1:36); "For God so loved the world that he gave his only son..." (3:16); "... if you do not believe that I am the one I claim to be you will indeed die in your sins" (8:24). Only by understanding the Jewish context of sacrifice can any reference to the Pascal lamb be fully understood.

The second startling transformation that occurs in the fourth Gospel concerns the early identification of Jesus with God. From the first paragraph and continuing throughout the narrative, Jesus is explicitly identified with God. The "I am" Hebrew saying is unmistakable in its obvious reference. Even the claims of Jesus are bolder and more provocative. For example, the passage in (8:16): "I stand with the Father, who sent me." And in (8:42): "If God were your Father, you would love me, for I came from God and now I am here. I have not come on my own; but he sent me."

Contrast this theme with Mark where Jesus explains to his disciples that the "secret of the kingdom of God has been given only to you" (4:11). To everyone else, the message would be conveyed through the use of parables to obfuscate their covert meaning. And Jesus gave them strict orders "not to tell who he was" (3:11).

The third important revision concerns the status of the Jews. They are now portrayed as wicked and children of the devil. The attempt is to place the murder of Jesus upon Jewish hands. Note the obvious reference: "You belong to your father, the devil, and you want to carry out your father's desire. He was a murderer..." (8:44).

In the dialogue with Pilate, the conversation between Jesus and Pilate appears to be between equals. Pilate appears reasonable. His questions legitimate. In fact, Pilate is portrayed as pleading with the crowd not to crucify Jesus. Repeatedly, the crowd insists upon crucifixion, but Pilate continually resists.

Jesus utters the prophetic words, "Therefore the one who handed me over to you is guilty of a greater sin" (19:11). The Jewish link to the death of Jesus had been sealed.

The fourth important theme is Jesus's demeanor on the cross. In Matthew and Mark, Jesus is portrayed as feeling disillusioned and abandoned. He is depicted as actually questioning why God has forsaken him. In John, the uncertainty has gone. Jesus awaits his faith with dignity and honor in order that the "Scripture would be fulfilled."

A: The Resurrection in John

In contrast to the other Gospels, John has Mary Magdalene going to the tomb on Sunday morning. Again, it is legitimate to ask why she should be going to the tomb after the body of Jesus had been embalmed with seventy-five pounds of myrrh and aloes. This is an enigma wrapped within a mystery.

Upon reaching the tomb, she discovers it empty. She proceeds to inform Peter and the other disciple. They both set out to see for themselves. Both men engage in a foot race to the tomb. What I find significant is that even though the beloved disciple reaches the tomb first, he waits for Peter before he goes into the tomb. This story, which appears only in John, clearly adumbrates the importance of Peter in the development of the church.

I also find the appearance of Mary Magdalene outside the tomb especially revealing. After Peter and the other disciple leave, Mary observes "two angels in white" where Jesus had laid. Recall that in Luke they had been portrayed as two men "in clothes that gleamed liked lightening." In Matthew, it had been one angel. And in Mark, it was merely "a young man dressed in a white robe." This escalating mythology is bewildering with its obvious embellishments. Note that the order is from mundane to more angelic appearances.

Thinking nothing unusual about the appearance of two angels, Mary proceeds to engage in an innocuous dialogue. She inquires about the location of Jesus. The suggestion in this passage would preclude resurrection appearances. Mary is claiming the right to the body of Jesus. But if she knew that Jesus arose with a resurrected body, why this anomalous claim?

Furthermore, while it isn't my purpose here to detail the full implication, it should be noted that in first century Judea only a wife could lawfully claim the body of a deceased.[1]

Subsequently, Jesus appears to his disciples. Apparently, one of the characteristics of this resurrected body is to go through doors. Jesus convinces Thomas after Thomas examines Jesus's wounds. The primacy of Peter is once again affirmed through Jesus's request that Peter "feed my sheep."

Chapter Seven: Resurrection: A Reconstruction

As I reread the Gospel narrative and the letters of Paul, I am amazed by the power of the story. If all the synoptic Gospels were written like John, the problem of literalization would not have been as obscure.

I think it is certain that the disciples had an experience. Midrash is the attempt to give understanding to that experience by incorporating the symbolism of the Hebrew texts. The symbols appropriated to the first century AD cannot be relevant to the 20th-century mind. In empirical matters, science must reign supreme.

However, the experience of the Resurrection (of Easter) transcends time and space. The validity of that experience lives on. The symbols that we use to translate that experience will vary with the scientific culture of the time.

Why do I affirm my belief that the disciples had an experience? Because their dramatic transformation demands nothing less. The entire Jewish contexts preclude self-fulfilling prophecies. The Jewish faith believed in a general resurrection at the end of time.

The resurrection of Jesus defied all their concepts for that understanding. The central core of this belief is that the disciples had a life-changing, transformative experience from cowards to martyrs. This is the one unexplained and unexplainable fact that cries out its truth.

But couldn't the resurrection have been fully concocted as so many other Bible stories appear to have been?

Christianity couldn't have been formed without the dedication and perhaps even death, of the disciples including Paul. What could explain the rapid rise of such a movement set against a hostile climate of political and religious oppression? To anyone that would argue otherwise, I offer this challenge: Show me a movement within history where people knowingly went to their death in support of a belief or cause that they knew to be false? We know from our own experiences that as death approaches, the usual tendency is to cleanse oneself of guilt.

The growth of Christianity testifies to the faith of its initial believers. Christianity was a movement within Judaism. As it began to break away around 80 AD, the conflicting and hostile forces at work were overwhelming.

On the one front, we find the various sects of Judaism as embodied in the Pharisees and Sadducees. On the other side, we find the might of Rome set against destroying the remnants of Jewish resistance.

These are undeniable facts of history. A movement—let alone a religion—doesn't quickly take roots in such an inhospitable environment. The tenacity and vigor of the disciples were heroic-beyond words.

We must keep in mind, the disciples were very ordinary people from all walks of life. Prior to the resurrection, they were depicted as cowards who forsook Jesus and fled. Why the change in attitude in them and Paul? How can we account for such life-transforming experiences?

Perhaps it was a hallucination. But this wasn't a passive experience. I don't believe that a hallucinatory image registering upon a passive mind offers sufficient explanation. The only experience that I could offer today that may be similar is the near-death experience.

Furthermore, hallucinations by their very definition are subjective in nature. That certain individuals could have such a life-changing experience would seem to argue against subjectivity.

The Bible narratives are so confounded with midrashic interpretation that it is impossible to give specifics. Did the life-changing experience happen individually or collectively? Could they happen individually and still be as powerful in their effect?

Rephrasing the latter option yields an immediate "yes." The experience of Paul clearly points to a subjective phenomenon. We have discussed Paul's usage of the Greek word *ophthe* in describing his revelation of Jesus. The historical reference is clearly to a vision, a subjective experience.[1]

Paul was even more emphatic in describing Jesus's glorified body as imperishable. On his journey to Damascus, the "men traveling with Saul–Paul–stood there speechless; they heard the sound but did not see anyone" (Acts 9:17).

This is clearly the most compelling account of a subjective experience transforming an individual. When I say "subjective" I mean to suggest that the experience could not be recaptured by recording instruments. For its manifestation was outside the boundaries of time and space.

Assuming the resurrection experience was something akin to a vision, would that make it any less valid? Is it possible for deceivers to establish a faith based on voluntary beliefs that dominate half the world?

The events surrounding the resurrection experience are ambiguous. However, their effect on history is indubitable. Again. the focus should be on the manifest behavior–before and after this personal encounter. All interpretations emanate from this ineffable experience.

I find it interesting that as interpretations are further removed from the resurrection experience, the greater the embellishment. For Paul, who was closest in terms of chronological time, he manages to express his faith in the resurrection in only four sentences (Cor 15:3-7). Mark writing a decade later expands this to eight verses. For Matthew, the geometric progression continues at twenty verses. And finally, for John, it consumes fifty-three verses[2].

Let us list the options open to us and exhaust their possibilities. From there the deductions will become more compelling.

First, we can say that the resurrection was a historical event that took place in approximately 33 AD. The Gospels are not a literal recording of those events.

On this point, we must be careful not to intermix faith with history. At the beginning of the book, I listed the historical facts about Jesus which rest on a solid foundation, beginning with being born around 4 BCE and ending with a community that was formed to await his return.

Was the Easter experience a literal event? Allow me to continue the initial analogy. I first began with: the witnessing of a UFO. We can extend the analogy even further. We find out that not only are the witnesses members of a UFO club, but we also learn that the aliens have appeared to only those individuals. Hence, membership gives rise to selective perception.

If the analogy was to end there, the belief in resurrection would be hard to tolerate. When we take note of the life-changing transformation that the Easter event symbolizes, then the analogy breaks down. The life-changing impact upon the disciples is the irreducible core upon which the foundation of Christianity is built.

There are simply too many inconsistencies and contradictions to try to harmonize. How many people went to the tomb after Jesus's death? Three in Mark, two in Matthew, at least four in Luke, and one in John.

When did Jesus proclaim himself to be the Messiah? Did Jesus's disciples expect his imminent return after his death? How many miracles did Jesus perform? Why was Jesus crucified? And so on.

These and so many other questions can lead the search into an endless excursion. We have enough information upon which we can draw meaningful conclusions.

We must consider the historical context and the symbolism for a fuller understanding. For example, in Mark, Jesus exorcises a possessed man. When Jesus asks his name, the reply is "Legion" (5:9).

The symbolism is too compelling to ignore. A legion was the symbol of Roman power and authority. In linking colonial domination with demonic possession, the political implications are obvious. A suppressed people always long for freedom and expulsion from their captors. However, political expression must take subtle and symbolic forms lest the ire of the existing authorities is aroused.

Hence, literalism excludes the rich symbolism that lies below the surface. For example, note the trial of Jesus before the Sanhedrin. The Gospel narratives read like eyewitness accounts. But who is recording these events? For as Mark noted, the disciples scattered after Jesus's death.

The second possibility is that the resurrection experience rests upon visions of individual persons. As such, they remain beyond objective verification. The report of eyewitnesses is to simply buttress the claim that something extraordinary happened.

Most Jewish scholars to the extent that they subscribe to any resurrection beliefs, consider this to be the most likely explanation.

Can visions alone account for the transformation of the apostles? And is that the meaning of Easter? Crossan writes, "What happened historically is that those who believed in Jesus before his execution continued to do so afterwards. Easter is not about the start of a new faith but the continuation of an old one. Despite his crucifixion, Jesus was for his followers alive, present, and empowering them to do the work of the kingdom still... Of course, there may have been visions and trances. There are always such in every religion, and I have no reason to think that Paul was alone in his. But the basic reality is that those whom Jesus empowered as healers and invited around an open table kept his vision and program alive, and continue to experience his presence in vision and program. That, to me, is Easter."[3]

Against this assessment, I ask: Is this realistic? Crossan is a brilliant and scholarly writer. I question this assessment not upon the altar of religious erudition for I would surely be at a disadvantage. But upon the bedrock of practical reason. Why the stark difference of the disciples before and after the resurrection? Perhaps we can attribute the difference to guilt. Do men go to their death to alleviate the sin of guilt? Is guilt a sufficient motivator to engender martyrdom?

Note that Crossan does acknowledge the experience of visions.But I must respectfully ask: Is even that sufficient? Whatever the experience was, words fail to describe this personal, transcendental encounter. All we can say is that "something," an ineffable experience, occurred that radically transformed certain individuals to the extent that they were willing to die for their beliefs.

In the words of E.P. Sanders, "That Jesus's followers (and later Paul) had resurrection experiences is, in my judgment, a fact. What the reality was that gave rise to the experiences I do not know."

"Much about historical Jesus will remain a mystery. Nothing is more mysterious than the stories of his resurrection, which attempt to portray an experience that the authors could not themselves comprehend."[4]

This is an honest assessment. Can history prove that there was a resurrection? Hardly! A transcendental experience is outside the boundaries of time and space. Just as so much of science is based upon inference, we must invoke a similar methodology to describe the religious experience. For example, we cannot observe the trajectory of electrons directly. Rather we infer their presence through residual tracks in a bubble chamber.

Similarly, we infer the power and reality of the resurrection through the experience of transformed lives. In behavioral terms, we can say that some stimulus x, produced an extraordinary response. I would argue that the phenomena produced were more than the passive registering of some incoming stimulus or vision. It was as if the experience radically changed their psychological beliefs and attitudes. And even today, such an experience would be tantamount to being called miraculous.

But who was Jesus? Was he the son of God? I find the need to anthropomorphize God disillusioning, I must say that I find it difficult to think of a perfect being as falling within our biological categories. If we don't have the God-language to talk about the resurrection experience, then surely, we don't have the words to talk about God. And yet, we freely project based upon our own limitations. For it serves to alleviate the uncertainty we feel in trying to express the inexpressible.

Who was Jesus? The words of Mahatma Gandhi resonate with meaning. "To me, he was one of the greatest teachers humanity has ever had. To his believers, he was God's only begotten son. Could the fact that I do or do not accept this belief have any more or less influence in my life? Is all the grandeur of his teaching and his doctrine to be forbidden to me? I cannot believe so... My interpretation...is that in Jesus's own life is the key to his nearness with God; that he expressed as no other could, the spirit and will of God. It is in this sense that I see and recognize him as the son of God."[5]

I am reminded of my earlier philosophical days in trying to reduce a thing to its essence. Take the example of the chair. It is a flat plane with usually four supporting legs. Of course, a three-legged stool could also be construed as a chair. Suppose we saw off another leg. Then another. And so on. At what point would the chair stop being a chair?

A Platonist would approach this from a different perspective. The concept chair derives its identity by participating in the eternal, immutable form of chairness. Hence, because a finite object (chair) participates in the eternal form (chairness), its essence can never be destroyed.

I go through this simple excursion to ask this question: What makes Jesus the Christ?

Is it the empty tomb? Is it his teachings? Is it how he lived his life? Is it that he died for our sins? Is it the resurrection experience? What particular aspect of Jesus's life gives him his unique Christian identity? Conversely, once we have identified that aspect of Jesus's identity, then its absence would necessarily negate that identity.

The church must open itself up to scholarly examination. The truth can be suppressed for only so long. I find it disconcerting to note that serious inquiry into the nature of Jesus dates back to the turn of this century starting with the great Protestant scholar Karl Ludwig Schmidt (1891-1956). For over 1800 years the church has suppressed open dialogue and debate on the divinity of Jesus,[6]

As recently as December 15, 1979, the great Belgian theologian, Edward Schillebeeckx, found himself summoned to appear before Rome's Congregation for the Doctrine of Faith to answer the questions about his unorthodoxy.[7] This was the same Vatican organization that in 1633 had condemned Galileo for correctly teaching that the earth revolved around the sun.

Schillibeeckx found himself on trial and his views on Jesus questioned. The message conveyed was unmistakable. Confine your scholarship within orthodox parameters. Transgress those boundaries at your peril.

Scholarship cannot flourish under these constraints. A faith that can be destroyed by historical scholarship isn't worthy of its name. Faith is buttressed by critical analysis.

In the final analysis, every person must find his own truth. The subjectivity of experience is paradoxically threatening and exhilarating. Threatening in that we are forced to find meaning amidst the chaos and challenge of our experience. Exhilarating in that once the search for meaning is obtained, our consciousness is elevated to a higher truth. Upon that perspective, we embrace the miraculous, marvel at the mysterious, and tolerate the uncertainty.

The central core of Jesus's identity was his resurrection. If there was no resurrection, then the status of Jesus would never have arisen. But we must not confuse symbols with experience. Just as we should not confuse the road map with the road.

The resurrection experience was an encounter with the divine. It is not about empty tombs, angels, or virgin births. These are first-century symbols used to describe an ineffable experience that burst upon their consciousness. "Death cannot contain him" was the battle cry. As the intensity of this experience began to be put in words, the embellishment of Jesus's divinity grew. By the time we reach the Gospel of John, Jesus is identified with God since the beginning of time.

We must separate the line of historical truth from the embellished myths of religious faith. If we accept Jesus's occupation as a carpenter, then he would have been part of the artisan class. As mentioned previously, the artisan class was among the lowest classes on the social scale except for the degraded and expendable classes.

Within this class, a certain cultural trajectory inevitably followed. Jesus was born and died a Jew. The society in which he lived profoundly influenced his beliefs. We must ask what the cultural expectations were in this era. It was common for a Jewish male to marry. The fact that the Bible portrays Jesus as celibate is a cultural deviation that needs to be explained rather than assumed.

It was also likely that Jesus was illiterate as was 95% of the Jewish state and 100% of the artisan class.

Was Joseph the father of Jesus? I believe that a strong case can be made that he wasn't. But, that is beside the point. Was Jesus married? Again the probability is high that he was. Cultural prescriptions are difficult to go against.

I would even concede the point offered by the Jesus Seminar that, at most, seventeen percent that is contained in the Gospels, are the authentic sayings of Jesus. Again, I would say that is irrelevant.

I would also concede that most of the miracles were a function of placebo effects. But again, I reiterate that this is beside the point.

Then what is the point? I can do no better than to quote Bishop Spong. "We can reject the literal narratives about the resurrection and still accept the truth and power of the resurrection event itself. That is the distinction that must be made. We would not have the legends unless there had been a moment so indescribable that legends became to explain it. We would not have an Easter tradition unless there had been an experience so real that earthbound words could not capture it. Easter points us to a dimension of life that became so visible that ecstatic silence was originally the only appropriate response."[8]

The resurrection experience is the symbolic dawning upon consciousness that "death could not contain him." The empty tomb is a symbol to contain the truth of the experience. In all cases, the experience gives rise to the interpretation of the symbols used to describe the event.

It would be incredible to believe that Jesus was singled out for special burial after experiencing such a humiliating death. I agree with Crossan that Jesus was buried by his enemies in a shallow grave that "made his body easy prey for scavenging animals."[9]

I find intriguing corroboration for this in all the thousands of people crucified by the Romans, only one has been recovered as evidence of crucifixion.[10]

It is true that the mundane trajectory that Jesus was on led on to political and religious persecution. As Spong mentions, "We had relativized the claims of the law, introduced competing values, broken the power of religious controls, and threatened the nature with religious anarchy."[11] In short, Jesus managed to make an enemy of everyone. Not because Jesus was malicious or evil, but because that is the price that any true revolutionary pays when changing the status quo.

The status quo consists of a delicate equilibrium of competing interests each tolerating the other factions to the extent they extract some payoff. Anyone that proposes to change the social dynamic is bound to encounter resistance and rebellion.

But a device needed to be invoked to set up the empty tomb scenario. If Jesus was buried, as is likely, by his enemies, then the dramatic climax could not be staged. If, on the other hand, Jesus was buried by his friends, then the foundation would be established.

That figure was embodied in the personage of Joseph of Arimathea. That a respectable member of the Sanhedrin world would voluntarily come forward and provide a royal burial to a condemned blasphemer is highly unlikely.

But whenever in doubt, look beyond the symbols. The death of Jesus meant the end of his movement. In the words of Mark, the disciples "all forsook him and fled."

Jesus was likely placed in a common grave. Burial removed the stench of decaying flesh. After a few days, unmarked bones remained.

I am amused by how often I have heard Christian literalists defend their faith by noting that if the tomb wasn't empty, then all the enemies of Jesus had to do was produce the body of Jesus as proof and the movement would have been destroyed instantly.

In a later chapter, I shall discuss Christian Apologetics for the resurrection. For now, I wish to note how absurd such a claim is. Would a few bone remnants convince anyone that Jesus had died? Furthermore, when a story deviates from its historical trajectory, that deviation should be justified and defended.

The problem with the Scriptures is that midrashic interpretation is confused with literal history. Literal history would not allow a Joseph of Arimathea to claim the body of Jesus. Such an event would have been scandalous and unprecedented. Furthermore, if it was literal history, then the very situation that the chief priests and Pharisees feared was brought about by giving the body to Joseph of Arimathea.

Furthermore, only John among the Gospel writers accords Jesus an honorable burial. According to Raymond Brown, an honorable burial included "trimming the hair, clothing the corpse, covering the head with a veil..."[12] While Brown acknowledges that it is difficult to ascertain how many of these customs were operative at the time of Jesus, a literal reading of John reveals that the body was wrapped with strips of linen along with a mixture of Myrrh and aloes" (John 19:39-40).

Brown's meticulous discussion continues by asking if there was sufficient time to buy the burial items. While in itself this is a legitimate question, I don't consider this the most important question. Jesus was convicted of blasphemy by the Sanhedrin on religious grounds. In the political arena, he was also convicted of being the "King of the Jews." The charge was treason. Does it make any sense to accord a condemned blasphemer and traitor an honorable burial?

Even Brown acknowledges that if Jesus was convicted of treason then "little indeed would be the likelihood that the priests of Judea would have given the body of crucified would be king to his followers for burial."[13]

There are several possibilities that need to be examined to the question: Was Jesus crucified under Roman or Jewish law? Or both?

As literal events, the scripture passages relapse into inconsistencies and contradictions. As symbols, they point to the greater reality of the experience.

I also believe that the figure of Judas Iscariot was a midrashic invention. I am still puzzled at what Judas- if indeed he existed- actually betrayed. The location of Jesus was well known. He had been preaching publicly and was well recognized.

Again, let us look at Judas from the perspective of symbolism. As the Gospel evolved, the betrayal of Jesus was increasingly bestowed upon the Jews. In the most dramatic depiction, Matthew writes, "Let his blood be on us and our children" (Matthew 27:25).

The name Judas is too close to the name "Judah," the nation, to simply dismiss as coincidence. We add the thirty pieces of silver in Zechariah (11:22). For Matthew, this constituted the fulfillment of the prophecy (Matthew 27:9-10).

Is it coincidental that in the story of Joseph and his brothers in the book of Genesis that the individual who betrays his brother is named Judah? All these separate elements unify under the rubric of midrashic interpretation. Again in all cases, we must transcend the symbols and ask what is the experience being pointed to? Let us go back and enter that first-century world with Jewish eyes and understanding.

With the death of Jesus, the movement splintered. The disciples, gripped by fear and uncertainty, became numb to the reality of Jesus's death. Those that had walked with him understood that his meaning was different than the image of a conquering hero from the House of David. Jesus's weapon was his wisdom. He preached a different message from all other alleged Messiahs. The message was not new. For the great Jewish Rabbi Hillel from less than a century before Jesus wrote, "whatever is hateful to you, do not do to your fellow man. This is the whole Law…"

Even after Jesus's death, I have described how his disciples still expected his return. But despite Jesus's departure, man's relationship with God would never again be the same. For Jesus had preached a brokerless relationship with God. That is, a relationship that could bypass the authority of the temple and be conducted directly with God.

If we look beyond the symbolism, the rending of the veil in Mark suggests this new development. The general function of a veil was to demarcate the holy place from the profane.

The tearing of the veil depicts the departure of God's presence. Hence, the death of Jesus means that the sanctuary no longer served its historical function.

In addition, in Matthew, the tearing of the veil is accompanied by darkness upon the whole land.

In general, the rending of the sanctuary veil is not only indicative of God's wrath but there is also a positive message: Jesus's death facilitated direct access to God. How? "Once a year the Jewish high priests went through the Katapetasma or veil that separated the Holy Place from the inner Holy of Holies; in the latter he incised the gold cover (Kapporet) of the Ark of the covenant and sprinkled it with the blood of the bull and goat previously sacrificed (Lev 16:11-19).

But we need to place this interpretation in context. Without the Jewish belief in sacrifice that we discussed earlier, the image of Jesus as the "Suffering Servant" loses any significance. Within that context, continuity and logic is preserved.

Hence, Jesus's crucifixion becomes symbolic of the paschal lamb. And since Jesus–by virtue of his divine status–was the perfect sacrifice, the continuation of the sacrificial ritual is obviated.

A: The Dawning of the Kingdom

I have found that some of Brown's analysis is cogent and powerful. The many signs given in the Gospels simultaneous with Jesus's death symbolize the inauguration of God's kingdom on Earth. Hence, the signs are clearly apocalyptic and signify the end of the world.

It is often overlooked that Jesus the Jew believed that God had chosen Israel among all nations to bestow his favor. Much of Jesus's teachings stress the relationship between God as the all-loving father and the individual. Whereas so much of Jewish history recounts the image of God as vengeful but just, Jesus's teachings emphasize God as a loving father.

In an earlier passage, I concluded that Jesus expected something dramatic to happen within his lifetime. After his death, his disciples expected Jesus to return. As events unfolded in defiance of this expectation, his arrival was postponed into the indefinite future.

As I survey these observations, I'm constantly reminded of Jesus's Jewish heritage. As a child, his impressionable mind was frequently exposed to numerous examples of God's intervention to save the world. The parting of the sea to save his people from the pursuit of the Egyptian army was vivid in his recollection. God was not only transcendent but also immanent.

The twelve tribes of Israel would be restored. God's glory would be bestowed upon the Jews.

The coming of the kingdom should not be interpreted as the final culmination of God's glory where the son of God gathers all nations to give dispensation to those who are to inherit God's kingdom. Rather, the apocalyptic signs surrounding Jesus's death are harbingers that if the kingdom of God had not fully arrived at least it had begun. Jesus's resurrection adumbrates the coming of the kingdom along with the general resurrection.

If Jesus was a descendant from the Jewish nation, his message would be universal. Remember how Jesus violated the laws of kosher and dined with Jews and

Gentiles alike. The kingdom of God was accessible to all. The confession by the centurion during Jesus's crucifixion is the beginning symbology that God's message should go out to all of the people.

B: Vision of Jesus

For Bishop Spong, whatever happened to define the Easter experience, Peter or Simon or Cephas took center stage. Was this vision objective? No, if we construe it to be an experience within time and space. I find it significant that the same word *ophthe* which is used in Isaiah's account of seeing God is the same word used by the disciples to describe their encounter with the Divine.

Isaiah's experience wasn't objective. Neither was Paul's. But each experience was no less real. The impact was profound. The transformation complete. I believe that the experience was a rendezvous with God. I didn't believe it is possible for people to go to their death for something that is a lie or they don't believe in.

At the very minimum, we can say that something happened after Jesus's crucifixion. Did it happen after three days? Unlikely and it doesn't really matter. According to Bishop Spong, Peter's vision happened six months after Jesus's death. The triumphant entry into Jerusalem wasn't by Jesus but by Peter after that transformational vision.[14]

I am saying that the entire edifice of the Jesus tradition rests upon the subjective foundation of mystical visions. And what about all the various elements of the poignant drama such as Judas, Joseph of Arimathea, virgin birth, empty tombs, the various miracles, and so on? Are they too concoctions?

The answer to both questions is a categorical "yes." We have confused the symbols with the experience. The map isn't the terrain but points us to it.

The story of Jesus will be retold to fit a modern context. The symbols we use may change. The experience remains immutable. A first-century mind may believe that epilepsy is caused by demon possession. Or that Jonas did spend three days and nights in the belly of a whale. Or that heaven lies above the clouds. Or that a female contributes nothing to the formation of a zygote.

First-century understandings must yield to the truths that science has confirmed. For example, I alluded to the power of near-death experience in producing radical changes in the people having the experience. In one seminar that I attended, the individual recounted his experience in which every atom in his body was filled with love. In his retelling of the episode, his words became strained and increasingly heavy. Finally, his emotions engulfed him as he began to break down and cry.

There is absolutely no doubt in my mind that what this person experienced was real. In recent times, our ability to resuscitate individuals has increased the experience of near-death. The problem is that there is no paradigm for dealing with such events.

My point is that the symbols we use today will be different than the symbols used to describe the resurrection experience in the first century AD. If we look at the elements of the passion story, most can be reconstructed from the Book of Zachariah, the Book of Malachi, Psalm 22 and 118, and Isaiah. Let us look at a few passages to appreciate the power of midrash:

1. "My God, my God, why hast thou forsaken me" (Psalm 22:1).
2. "...they divided my garments among them and for raiment they cast lots' (Psalm 22:18).
3. "He was afflicted, yet... like a sheep before her shearers is silent, so he did not open his mouth" (Isaiah 53:7).
4. "...He protected all bones, not one of them will be broken" (Psalm 34:20).

I have already made reference to the thirty pieces of silver, cleansing of the temple, riding into Jerusalem on the back of a donkey, etc. Are these all coincidences? I have argued that it is too farfetched to argue that it's the fulfillment of prophecy.

I would claim that these are midrashic interpretations to give form to a powerful and ineffable experience.

C: Jesus - Son of God

But was Jesus really the son of God? My short answer is "yes" with the caveat: so are we all. Part II of the book will be to examine the nature of God. But for now, I wish to note that to the extent Jesus is human, his death is more real to me. I'm not impressed with Jesus's agony in the Garden of Gethsamane. How genuine was Jesus's sacrifice if he knew that the pain and suffering would be fleeting?

To the extent that Jesus was human then his death is more meaningful and genuine.

As I mentioned earlier, the evolution of Jesus's divinity culminated in the Gospel of John with Jesus existing from the beginning and having equivalent status to God. If Jesus and God are the same, then God is sacrificing himself to atone for our sins. I find such claims preposterous.

Jesus was divine, and so are we all. The spark of the divine resides within each of us. The greatness of Jesus lies not in his alleged status nor in the originality of his teachings. The truth lies in the understanding of our nature with God. The kingdom of God is within us. For our soul is part of the divine. Jesus is a bridge across that wide gulf that separates us from our divine nature.

Jesus's egalitarianism and unbrokered relationship with God constitute powerful expressions of that message. If all of us are spiritual creatures, then we are all equal in the eyes of God. The bodily vehicle that we use as an abode for the spirit should not be the focus. The proper emphasis should be on the inner kingdom that we all possess and how it may lead us to our divine salvation.

If Jesus was literally the son of God, then how much weight do we place on his deeds? How genuine is it to suffer less than three days knowing that physical resurrection awaits you? And the phrase "That God gave his only begotten son to save us from our sins" I consider nothing short of ridiculous.

For me, speaking very personally, this literalism is stifling. He has turned me away from organized religion. A God that plays these kinds of games isn't worthy of worship. A God that demands worship isn't perfect. A God that takes sides in human affairs is dangerous and arbitrary.

Those who accept the notion that God intervenes at certain points in history should ask the causes for the intervention. Why did God intervene two thousand years ago but not during the Holocaust?

Who is God for me? In part two of this book, I shall dwell upon this question at length. For now, I wish to observe that the most we can say about God is to use Tillich's phrase that God "is the inexhaustible ground of all being." I don't believe that we have the right to say that God is omniscient, omnipotent, perfect, or has a particular sex.

And who is Jesus for me? Jesus was a charismatic faith healer and a Mediterranean Jewish peasant. Even though I would challenge the authenticity of the overwhelming majority of the teachings attributed to him in the Gospels, I believe that there is enough there to point the way.

Jesus understood the special relationship we all have with God. The spirit of the loving God resides within each of us. That is why Jesus preached an unbrokered relationship with God and a radical egalitarianism.

We need not concoct torturous stories to explain what happened. As I explained earlier, the status quo is a function of competing interests sharing some benefit. Jesus's message was threatening not only to the Romans but to the Sanhedrin as well.

Jesus's ideas were revolutionary to the social order. Only a revolutionary could make the kind of impact that Jesus did. In his heart, he knew the genuineness of his convictions and the truth of his message. At any point, he could have easily saved himself from crucifixion.

The fact of Jesus's humanity only enhances the power of this message. As a human being, I can relate to him more effectively and use the power of his actions to guide me in my relationship with God.

Chapter Eight: Conclusion

To a large extent, we can say that reality is a social reconstruction. Technically speaking, the perception of our everyday world is merely reflected light. All objects reflect light, i.e., have albedo. When you see a cup, what you are really seeing is light reflecting from a cup. The light enters our eyes, goes through visual pathways, and enters the visual cortex. In the brain, that light is intermingled with our beliefs, prejudices, and emotions to give rise to the object of perception. This is not a passive process, hence, my rationale for viewing reality as a reconstruction.

I believe that we can be sure that all of us view the world differently. Fortunately, there are enough points of similarity to allow us to talk about a shared reality. Similarly, I view life as fundamentally subjective. The pain I feel in my back is my pain. Emotional experiences in general are unique and singular. Hence, it becomes difficult to employ language to convey the meaning of the emotional reality.

Most of the language we employ deals with man's other nature namely, the intellect. We use our intellect to further the cause of science. In that realm, logic pervades the world.

In the realm of emotions, reality is no less real. In fact, we may say that its impact upon us is even more real. For example, isn't it ironic that for all the wonders we attribute to the cerebral cortex (intellect), we give predominant status to the limbic system (emotions) when making decisions concerning personal relationships?

Each realm employs different tools to convey the experience. In science, we know that experimental bias will contaminate the outcome. Hence, the intellect must become detached from bias.

In the emotional realm, the psyche becomes more enmeshed in its poignant phenomenology. The story gains force in its retelling.

The success of science has blinded us to the other emotional side. We need to develop a hermeneutics of this relatively unexplored part of ourselves.

As a starting point, I would posit that each experience has certain consequences or effects. The causal order would be the perception or the experience. Then the concomitant response or consequences. To be sure perceptions are necessarily subjective. The response or consequences is our linkage to reality.

Let's take one representative example. In the book *The Journey Home-What Near Death Experiences and Mysticism Teaches Us About the Gift of Life*, Phillip Berman recounts the following story. "If there was some way to do a psychological profile of me before and after my experience, there would be two different people, two very different personalities. I lost my fear as a result of my experience. I lost my sense of being worthless. I came back with a great sense of self-worth, self-love, and a tremendous amount of faith. Now I love people, I love being alive and I love having fun being alive, with all its places and means."[1]

Rather than dismiss the power of this experience, I would affirm its validity. To the extent that the experience changes the individual, then both criteria are satisfied.

The reality of subjective experience is so pervasive that we often take it for granted. If you went to the optometrist's office, your subjective experiences govern. So, too, with opinion polls, survey results, medical examinations, etc. In part, science couldn't function without appreciating the subjectivity of experiences within a limited context.

However, when we apply this paradigm to religion, it is conveniently dismissed. An encounter with some extraordinary manifestation is treated with suspicion. If I see a blinding white light and interpret that experience as an encounter with God, that experience is real to me.

I understand that the light can be construed as some cosmic rorschach. And in the process, may reveal some hidden truths about myself. But the reality of this subjective experience cannot be dismissed.

In fact, I would expect the near-death experience, revelations, or any mystical encounter to be heavily influenced by cultural beliefs. But again, the reality of the experience is affirmed.

In recent years, many attempts have been made to dismiss these types of experiences as a function of anoxia or some chemical imbalance. Again, I would say that whatever the cause, the experience is so powerful and life-changing that it merits further study.

Furthermore, I would caution that those who dismiss these experiences may be closing the door to an important dimension of human understanding.

I understand that presuppositions are going to slant the discussion. That is, if a person believes in the preexistence of a soul then any evidence is redundant. If on the other side, their starting point is epiphenomenalism i.e., consciousness is a byproduct of cellular interaction, then no proof is sufficient.

At the very minimum, I would err on the side of having an open mind. It is obvious that complexity and change govern our existence. A drop of water is a universe unto itself. I feel humbled and awed by the power of nature. I feel a certain reverence for the life I was born into. In my journey of a thousand miles, I've only begun my first step.

There is so much we still don't know. How do cells interact to produce consciousness? How does consciousness interact with matter? Is consciousness affected by the law of cause and effect? If so, then how is it that a causal chain can produce consciousness and then transcend the principle of causality? If the brain produces consciousness, then how much of the brain can we destroy without impairing consciousness? Can we artificially induce life-changing experiences? Is the belief in God across all religions a product of our aloneness in a hostile and indifferent universe?

There is so much we have learned. But even more is undiscovered. Inquiry is open to those who don't close the doors to further discovery. I don't know if there is a parallel universe, but I want to be open to that reality. The universe is pregnant with complexity. Its vastness overwhelms us. To those who harbor presuppositions that certain lines of inquiry are closed to further examination, then I would submit that science cannot escape its own metaphysics.

We presuppose that the world is an orderly place. We invoke the principle of induction to justify that unscientific leap. But how can we jump from part to whole?

The scientific enterprise, grounded upon the law of cause and effect, leads us to inescapable determinism. If people are governed by antecedent causes, then how can we hold people accountable for their actions?

As much as we hate to admit it, in our scientific age, metaphysics undergirds our science. The limitations of science necessarily carry us into the realm of metaphysics. Metaphysics places limits upon the hubris of science to explain everything.

Furthermore, metaphysics takes us into the realm of faith. But it need not be a blind faith buttressed mostly with dogma. Rather, a rational faith should be open to any possibilities and challenges. For example, the redshift hypothesis that galaxies are receding from us at the speed of light is mind-boggling. Big Bang cosmology challenges the steady state theory of the universe. The universe is a more complex place than we ever dreamed, and the scale of complexity occurs at all levels from the micro to the macro. In our quest to understand these complex phenomena, we'll learn more about ourselves.

Perhaps our conclusion will take us back to our starting point. Jesus's words ring with profound truth: The Kingdom of God is within. We can never know for certain. The rules of the game have been set up to allow room for faith. But I don't agree with Bertrand Russell's conclusion that the cards are stacked against a belief in God. The atheist requires at least as much faith as the theist, as I shall argue in the next section.

The so-called mystical experience is as old as recorded history. I am thoroughly impressed by its life-changing and transformational nature. How arrogant it is for anyone to deny the reality of that experience to someone who has undergone its impact. Especially so since experiences or consciousness is fundamentally subjective.

If Jesus is someone whose heightened consciousness enables me to reach out and bridge the gulf that separates us from the Divine, then I accept Jesus. To the extent that he was born a man in destitute conditions with no formal education, his status is enhanced. For if Jesus, given his limited social circumstances, could understand his relationship with God, then what about the rest of us blessed with more elevated material status? We stand upon the shoulders of giants. Humanity is a causal link in the evolutionary process.

We stand inspired and ready to reach out to the heavens in our upward thrust to make contact with the Divine. Based upon Jesus's teachings we learn that the journey is within. That in learning about ourselves, we are making contact with God.

Chapter Nine: Josh McDowell Revisited

When I started this journey several years ago, I had no idea where the destination would take me. But my search for the truth compelled me to move forward!

I have no financial stake in the ultimate success of this manuscript. As I learned a long time ago, material things are ephemeral and in a real sense, they control us as much as we derive pleasure from their use.

I have no ulterior motive for writing this book. I simply wanted to understand the roots of my childhood beliefs. I was brought up a Catholic. I went to Catholic school in the seventh and eighth grades.

My journey has been necessarily limited by the reality of my responsibilities with work. However, I'm humbled by the fact that there are people who devote their entire lives to searching for the historical Jesus. I am not one to spend my whole life searching one issue. I like to dig many different holes rather than one deep one. But I feel I've barely scratched the surface in tackling such an important question as the nature of Jesus.

When I began this journey, I was so interested and fascinated by individuals who started out as skeptics but later converted through their own research. In my quest, I was guided by their efforts. For purposes of this section, I will confine my comment to one prominent Christian writer namely, Josh Mcdowell(JM). JM was an initial skeptic who later became a convert. A sizable body of works attests to this conversion.[1]

I want to retrace the footsteps of JM to try to understand why his research led to such radically different conclusions than mine.

Point One: One basic difference is that JM considers the Bible as historically accurate. Hence, a literal interpretation is justified.

I addressed this particular point previously, but it bears repeating. The New Testament writers were believers. Believers are not neutral observers!

Furthermore, Jesus's resurrection appearances were confined to believers. In Acts, we are told that Jesus allegedly appears for forty-days after his resurrection. I find it compelling that no non-Christian sightings were made. Whether these appearances occurred in Jerusalem or Galilee, it is difficult to believe that no other non-Christian confirmatory references are cited.

Secondly, I must say that JM's citations of non-Christian references are flimsy at best. I appreciate JM's honesty in acknowledging that Josephus's passage in Antiquities that Jesus "was the Messiah" is a Christian insert.[2]

At best, the few paragraphs in which Josephus refers to Jesus simply attest to (1) Jesus's existence, (2) that Jesus was apparently charismatic enough to have followers, and (3) he was crucified under Pontius Pilate.

Any other conclusions beyond these historical facts are in the realm of speculation.

When we go beyond the writings of Josephus in search for more extra-biblical evidence for Jesus, the writings become even more scanty. I find it astonishing that Jesus- the Jew is hardly mentioned in any Jewish writings. JM notes that a large number of Jewish manuscripts were confiscated by the Roman authorities and burned. Furthermore, any reference to Jesus engendered a potential target of attack from both Roman and Christian authorities,

A sizable body of Jewish literature has been handed down to us through the ages. I find it incredible that Jesus who is portrayed as greater than Moses and Elijah should be so conspicuously absent.

In general, I would say that if one is looking for indubitable non-Christian testimony for some of the miraculous stories of Jesus, then they are going to be sadly disappointed.

Thirdly, I would make a more important point. Why take the approach that the Gospel writers were writing literal narratives? The span of time of the Synoptics is about one year. John stretches the period to three years. Doesn't it seem strange to write a biography on someone and only include one to three years of their life? In addition, the evidence of midrash is compelling. Even the NT writers make overt references to the Old Testament.

The symbolism is never appreciated. The Jewish context is ignored. And from that fabric we are supposed to weave an accurate portrayal of Jews.

Does anyone believe that Jesus ascended to heaven like Mary Poppins defying gravity? Or that Jesus was born to a virgin woman but that his ancestry is preserved through Joseph's lineage? Or that the healing of the demon-possessed man in Mark was really named Legion? I find the literalism stifling. Its perspective narrow. And its explanation leaves me frustrated.

However, I accept some historical truths in the NT. I earlier quoted the archeologist Sir William Ramsay. But the issue isn't literalism versus symbolism or midrash. The truth often lies in the middle path that permits the integration of these two diverse threads.

Point Two: "A vast network of multiplication sprung from Jesus and the first apostles. If any had included historical errors in their reports, the early literature would reflect controversy over matters of fact concerning what actually took place."[3]

An argument from silence is never determinative. It's like saying that because no one challenges the writing of a certain cult, then their teachings must be prima facie true.

Consider the fact that over 95% of the population was illiterate. The Jewish writings that JM so aptly explained as likely to be destroyed could very well have made reference to the Christian sect. But you can't have it both ways. That is, you can't justify the absence of Jesus's references in Jewish writings because of their possible destruction and argue the above quote.

I want to quote JM in his own words. "...The earliest writers appealed to eyewitnesses who could confirm or deny facts... They had nothing to gain by spreading lies."[4]

I find this passage ridiculous in content, preposterous in its implications. If you are trying to bolster belief in your cause, then attestations outside your circle of believers are critical. I've already mentioned that paucity of data outside the Christian writers.

Furthermore, to frame this discussion in terms of lying or not lying is a distortion. A powerful experience had gripped the apostles. We can only speculate upon the nature of that experience. But we can say that behaviorally the change was profound. Within the Jewish context, the Gospel writers struggled to understand the power of that experience. The OT had for years served to give interpretation to the sacred. Hence, the Gospels are their attempt to provide meaning to a metaphysical experience.

Misinterpretation occurs when we fail to understand the intention of the authors. Midrash was the attempt to explain the life of Jesus based on OT prophecy.

Point Three: Concerning the reliability of the Biblical records, I accept the Bibliographical test.[5] I can also appreciate the internal evidence tests, but my conclusion would be different. Is it consistent that an individual that was sentenced to death for treason by the political authorities and accused of blasphemy by the religious leaders be accorded a royal burial? Is it reasonable that the Gospel writers would offer so much data to show that Jesus was a descendant from the Davidic line with all its attending implications- only to later change the paradigm to Isaiah's Suffering Servant? Incidentally, only in the Dead Sea Scrolls do we find reference to the Anointed One, i.e., the Christ emerging from a priestly line. Is it reasonable to stretch the meaning of Isaiah (7:14) to provide relevance to the virgin birth of Jesus?

If literal understanding is our model, then how do we explain that between Abraham and Jesus, there are fifty-six generations? Matthew only accounts for forty-one.

Luke's genealogy is equally unconvincing. Between Abraham and Jesus, we have to account for a time period of 1,750 years. But Luke only accounts for thirty-seven generations. That is hardly enough to bridge the gap.

In general, on the internal evidence test, I have found the NT contradictory and inconsistent. I don't believe that invoking this criterion does anything to bolster the view of Christian Apologetics.

Pertaining to the external evidence tests, I would grant some corroboration with archeological findings. I'm particularly impressed with the finding that perfume bottles had long necks. At the Feast of Bethany, Jesus is reclining at a table. A woman with an alabaster jar of very expensive perfume breaks the jar and pours the perfume on Jesus's head. It has puzzled historians that the Greek term used in the passage literally means to "break" or "smash." Apparently, the archeological finding confirms that one literally had to break the jar to empty its contents.

The description of the geography and antiquities conforms to the archeological record. The burial of Jesus is less convincing. Of all the thousands of victims of crucifixion, we have recovered only one vestige. Two thousand rebels were crucified following three major messianic uprisings in 4 BCE. Why so few remnants if crucifixion was so widespread? Could it be that the method of burial in common graves allows beasts of prey such as carrion crows and scavenger dogs to further the indignity by dismembering the body?

Point Four: As I mentioned previously, this is the most compelling point that JM makes concerning the status of Jesus. I cannot dismiss this piece of evidence. If A = the disciples' pre-resurrection behavior, B = the experience, and C = the disciples' post-resurrection behavior, then clearly C can only be explained by B. Even behavioral psychologists- whose treatment of the mind as a black box, would have trouble explaining such a radical difference in behavior.

I don't believe that such an abrupt transformation occurred on the third day. That is symbolism. Bishop Spong believes that the moment of truth referred to as the Easter experience occurred to the disciples perhaps as long as three years after the death of Jesus.

We can deduce from this profound impact that Jesus was an extraordinary person. Upon the death of a dear friend or teacher, the mind struggles to understand. The disciples recollected how Jesus would embrace children, the lepers, and the sick. In Jesus, they saw something that can be labeled Divine. Jesus spoke intimately about the relationship with his father–abba (literal translation:daddy). This relationship was understood to be direct and unmediated. The Torah or Law was designed to serve man, not the reverse. His confidence allowed him to transcend kosher laws and dine with non-Jews.

In short, in Jesus, they saw someone who was fully alive. Unchained to the past and liberated to a future of infinite possibilities. His message seemed to transcend death itself. Jesus' message echoed in their minds and pervaded their existence. In that sense, Jesus was still alive!

We cannot be certain how this particular transformation took place. We cannot even be certain if it took place in Jerusalem or Galilee. What we can be certain of is that of the reconstituted disciples, only John died a natural death. The rest died cruel deaths for something they believed in.[6] What kind of belief could sustain such martyrdom? And what kind of experience could change a person so completely?

To dispose of these questions lightly is to miss a dimension of the human experience. For surely that which transforms one's worldview could be said to be more real than the mundane experiences that our minds encounter daily. Is not that which permanently endures just as important as fleeting sensory experience? We cannot invent an ontology based upon the length of our experiences. In the realm of experience, both the subjective and objective are equally real.

What I find so astonishing about this transformation was that it was so unexpected. I've learned about the power of self-fulfilling prophecies. Expectations condition our reality. In a group setting, those expectations can be further magnified until the belief becomes manifested.

But as I mentioned previously, the Jewish cultural belief was in a general resurrection at the end of time. I take seriously Crossan's hypothesis[7] according to Paul. Within this context, some trigger was needed to launch the cascade of subsequent events.

If I was pressed on the point of whether the appearance of Jesus was objective or subjective, I would reply, in all probability, the latter. But I would quickly add that it doesn't really matter. In the final analysis, a life-changing experience is no less real because of its subjectivity. The behavior before and after the experience becomes the connecting link to an objective methodology that demands a verdict..

My conclusions about Jesus are based in part on Paul's use of the Greek word *ophthe*. As previously noted, a good translation of this word would be "appeared to or was revealed to."[8] I think that there is little doubt that Paul's experience was that of a vision. In equating his own experience in which he never claimed to meeting Jesus with the disciples that accompanied Jesus, the circle becomes complete.

A: Evidence From Historical Geography

According to Josephus, a census did take place between 6-7 CE under the reign of Quirinius. However, that census only covered Galilee, not Judea. There is no corroborative evidence in secular records anywhere of a worldwide census ordered by the Roman emperor.[9] Furthermore, the time of Herod's death is placed at 4 BCE. In general, most scholars synchronized Jesus's birth with Herod's death. Hence, at the time of the census, Jesus would have been ten years old.

The Greek text of Luke 2:2, according to JM, can be interpreted as "This census is the first one coming to pass when Quirinius is ruling Syria."[10] Hence, the absence of the definite article "the" seems to indicate that Luke is referring to earlier and less known census dated around 5 BCE.

My question would be: What would be the purpose of having two annual back-to-back censuses? It must be understood that the census ordered by Quirinius in 6-7 CE provoked a rebellion. The taking of a census was an unpopular undertaking and fraught with peril. To the captive people, such an act could only serve to heighten the realization of their captivity. In such a setting, emotions are bound to run deep. Only the fuse needs to be lit to give vent to the people's suppressed rage.

Judea did not come under direct Roman rule until at least 6 CE. In general, the Roman policy towards Judea was designed to pacify religious convictions. Only in Judea did the coins not bear the emperor's face. It is even recorded that at times the Roman legion would bypass Judea to avoid offending Jewish sensibilities by displaying imperial portraits.[11]

Under this context, why would the Roman authorities purposely provoke a confrontation knowing that a census was unpopular at best?

Furthermore, women in the Jewish culture were considered mere chattel. In Exodus 20:17 women are deemed more valuable than servants, ox, and donkey. Yet, they were less valuable than a man's house.

JM acknowledges that Roman custom usually dictated that the census be conducted based upon "land ownership, not on home towns."[12] Then he uses an ancient papyrus dating around 104 AD as setting the historical precedent on requiring captive people to return to their city of origin. Again my question would be: why? The analogy is similar to my registering in Akron, Ohio when I live in Columbus, Ohio. What political or economic purpose is served through this anomalous arrangement?

If we accept the importance of Jewish prophesy that a Davidic Savior would emerge from Bethlehem (Micha 5), then Luke's torturous reasoning becomes more acceptable.

Between Bethlehem and Nazareth is a distance of ninety-three miles. What would be the purpose of taking a pregnant woman in her ninth month through such an arduous journey riding on a donkey? Is this plausible?[13]

To further his hypothesis, JM cites Adolph Deissmann—a German scholar—on finding an Egyptian papyrus dating 104 AD which required the Egyptians to return to their home city for the Roman Census in Egypt.[14]

This is a remarkable claim! Considering women were not allowed to own property, what would be the purpose of such an edict? More importantly, how would it be enforced?

I was so bothered by this passage that I went to Deissman's book directly. The relevant edict reads, "The enrollment by household being at hand, it is necessary all who for any case so ever are outside their nomes to return to their domestic hearths; that they may accomplish the customary dispensation of enrollment and steadfastly in the husbandry that belongeth to them."[15]

Let's define a few terms. "Nomes" pertains to province. "Husbandry" could signify farming or management of domestic affairs. "Hearths" could mean home.

How far outside the province did one have to return to his original home? If one was a thousand miles away, would the edict still apply? What about a hundred miles?

According to Josephus, we know that there was a census in 6 CE when Quirinius was legate. However, the census applied to people in Judea, Samaria, and Idumaea. Galilee was semi-independent and would not have been subject to the census. By semi-independent, I mean that Rome "governed remotely, being content with the collection of tribute and the maintenance of stable borders; for the most part, it left even these matters in the hands of loyal local rulers and leaders."[16]

A useful model to view this state of affairs is the Soviet empire after World War II. Each country in Eastern Europe employed some measure of autonomy.

However, when the Soviet hegemony was threatened then military intervention was used to preserve the communist order.

Similarly with the Roman occupation of Judea. Herod had been a supporter of Rome. For his loyalty, he was rewarded by being promoted to King of Judea in 37 BCE.

Herod died in 4 BCE. From 4 BCE to 30 CE, Galilee was ruled by Herod's son, Antipas.

I repeat this historical background because it is so necessary to understand Luke's reference to census taking. I find it interesting that Luke is the only Gospel to mention a census at the time of Jesus. And the reason is simple. Luke has to find a way to bring Jesus to Bethlehem to fulfill the prophecy.

Furthermore, it was usually the census takers that would travel. The objective was to connect the land and land owners for tax purposes. Land ownership was the principal means of wealth. Hence, a plausible interpretation of the edict was to urge people to return to their province to facilitate enrollment when the census takers arrived.

Even if taken at literal value, Luke's story shows blatant ignorance of the ordeal facing a woman in the ninth month of pregnancy.

For Matthew, no such problem exists. The holy family is already in Bethlehem. However, they leave Bethlehem in to avoid Herod's orders of killing "all the boys in Bethlehem and its vicinity who were two years old and under" (Matthew 2:16). But while the family is fleeing to Egypt, Luke has the family performing the ritual act of circumcision on the eighth day in Bethlehem and presentation to the temple on the fortieth day in Jerusalem (Luke 2:21-22).

These accounts are irreconcilable! What I find disturbing is that no other model besides the literal one is employed to interpret the events in the gospels. I would accept the minor points, as stated by JM that Luke's use of titles was probably correct. I would further grant that the listing of the towns that Jesus visited was probably correct.

But the explanation for Jesus cursing the fig tree in Mark 11 is not so easily accepted. How does JM explain this obscure passage? "Since the tree contained no fruit, Jesus seems to have used it as an object lesson to warn against professing something by our appearance but having no fruit to back it up."[17]

It is amazing to me how a literal interpretation could make possible such contorted explanations. The fig tree bears its fruit in September and October. The text makes clear that "it was not the season for the figs." Could a deeper meaning lie beneath these words?

Crossan offers one possible interpretation.[18] The context is critical. In the next passage after Jesus curses the fig tree, Jesus is overturning the tables of the money changers in the temple. Both actions are symbolic but the meaning is the same.

The conduct of the money-changers was absolutely essential to the functioning of the Temple. Jewish law and custom demanded sacrifice to balance the treasury of merit. Sacrifices were an important way to accumulate virtue as a balance against excess sin.[19]

Crossan suggests that the overturning of the tables of the money-changers was a symbolic act. "As the useless fig tree was destroyed, so symbolically was the useless temple."[20]

Another plausible interpretation is possible. The fig tree symbolizes and adumbrates the divine judgment. Those that lack faith will wither and die. Those who have faith will partake in the Kingdom of God.

I find it interesting to note the evolution of the fig story. Matthew includes the passage but Jesus's curse causes the tree to wither immediately. Luke omits the story and substitutes the parable of the fig tree. We do not know if this story had a common oral tradition. In the Synoptics, we have three different trajectories of a common story. In all instances, literalism fails us in understanding the symbolic meaning behind the words.

B: Mustard Tree Analogy

According to JM, the mustard tree still grew in Israel and can attain a height of fifteen feet. It never dawned on him to question the validity of his analogy.

The mustard tree can, at best, grow into a bush or shrub. It emits a pungent smell and grows wildly. In short, it is very much like a weed.

The proper analogy would've been to use the cedar tree whose sprawling and lofty branches majestically project into the skies. But why the curious analogy of likening the kingdom of God to a mustard bush?

I agree with Funk's suggestion that Jesus "parodies the mighty cedar by turning it into a weed."[21]

The Kingdom of God isn't a utopia. Rather you have to take the good with the bad to appreciate its meaning. A garden doesn't bear fruit without weeds. In controlling the weeds, we appreciate the harvest that much more.

C: Archeological Evidence

Why is it that out of all the thousands of people crucified by the Romans, only one set of bones was found to attest to the Roman practice of crucifixion? Could it be that the final cruelty of crucifixion was that scavenging animals left nothing to bury? And yet, I am perplexed by individuals like JM who appropriate one meaning to their story from available evidence only to miss the overall significance of the archeological findings.

D: The Miracles

When we try to understand any phenomenon, the context is critical. In the culture in which Jesus lived, the spiritual was believed to interpenetrate the physical world. Hence, it was commonly accepted that the spiritual could interact with the physical in tangible ways.

What was the reason for Jesus's ability to heal? Was it because of his alleged divine status? And yet, Jesus acknowledged that other Jews of his time could perform similar miracles. The wall between the natural and spiritual was porous. The presence of spirits was widely accepted. That is why spirit possessions necessitated exorcisms.

There are two types of miracles that Jesus performed: healing miracles and nature miracles. Let's elaborate upon each of these.

Healing miracles revolve around restoring a person to health or restoring a bodily function that was previously inoperative. For example, in Mark 7:31-37 a man "who was deaf and could hardly talk is brought to Jesus. Jesus proceeds to go through a ritual in which he spits and touches the man's tongue and ears. Jesus shouts "ephphatha" which literally means "be open." The man begins to speak plainly and to hear."

Hence, it becomes more plausible as to how Jesus could develop a reputation as a magician. This early miracle incorporates themes of magic. To differentiate Jesus from other faith healers and magicians, Matthew and Mark purposely omit any reference to incantations and the like.

The most prominent form of healing mentioned in the Synoptic Gospels is exorcisms. In Mark 9:17, Jesus heals a boy who seems to be suffering from epilepsy. Jesus proceeds to exorcise the spirit within the boy and cures him of his convulsions.

Pertaining to the nature miracles, they relate to such stories as calming a storm at sea or feeding the multitude.

The question that arises in my mind is: if Jesus did in fact perform all the miracles attributed to him by the disciples, why didn't he have more followers? We are told in Mark that Jesus admonishes his disciples not to tell anyone. But yet in a different vein, everywhere he went the crowds were overwhelming.

Reflect upon the scene of Jesus's triumphant entry into Jerusalem. In the trial before Pontius Pilate, Pilate asks the crowd to choose between Jesus and Barabbas. The crowd makes the incredible choice in picking Barabbas. If the objective of the Sanhedrin was to preserve the social order, then releasing Barabbas was contradictory to that goal.

It must be noted that the Sanhedrin had approximately twenty thousand temple servants and eighteen thousand workmen.[22] Hence, managing a particular outcome was possible. But was this a monolithic group? Had they not seen the public miracles of Jesus? Was their faith so blinded by the implications of Jesus's stature that they failed to see with their eyes? And was Barabbas really less threatening to the social order than Jesus?

I mention these concerns because I don't believe that the premise, as mentioned in the Gospels, leads to the desired conclusions.

Were any of the miracles a product of psychosomatic cures? The placebo effect is still with us today. Is it reasonable to assume that it was much more prevalent in an age of relative ignorance? And is epilepsy really a function of demon possession? We have been that the cultural climate in which Jesus lived was receptive to the occurrence of miracles. The power of self-healing works well within such fertile soil.

I mentioned earlier the trouble with translating certain words. For example, the term "leper" did include skin diseases such as psoriasis, eczema, and fungal infections. Skin diseases in turn included a social stigma. What if Jesus cured the illness, i.e., the social stigma, but not the disease within the body? Crossan writes, "I presume that Jesus, who did not and could not cure that disease or any other one healed the poor man's illness by refusing to accept the disease's ritual uncleanness and social ostracization."[23]

I find this a very useful distinction. The point of the story is to make the Kingdom of God accessible to even the marginalized and the disenfranchised. Hence, the kingdom is available to all of God's children.

What is the significance of the miracle stories? It is interesting that despite being direct witnesses, the disciples still didn't believe. In Mark14:48 we read that everyone deserted him and fled. It took the resurrection experience for them to believe that Jesus was the Messiah.

Recall the story of when John the Baptist is in prison and asks Jesus through his messenger if Jesus is the one they have been expecting? Jesus makes references to his miracles as a sign that prophecy has been fulfilled in him.

However, in Mark we see Jesus cautioning his disciples to keep his miraculous feats a secret. Is this history? Or is it prophecy historicized? In Isaiah 35:5 we read, "Then will the eyes of the blind be opened and the ears of the deaf unstopped. Then will the lame leap like a deer and the mute tongue shout for joy."

In the final analysis, we must remember that the miracle stories are recounted by believers in the faith. Their objectivity is necessarily compromised. I find it incredulous that with so many alleged public displays of the miraculous, there isn't any available evidence from a non-Christian source to independently attest to the validity of Jesus's miracles.

Chapter Ten: Josh McDowell's Meaning of Resurrection
A: On Paul's Perspective

I find it interesting that Paul's conversion to Christianity happened "within two or three years of Jesus's death."[1] JM quotes Professor James Dunn to buttress this claim.

However, it is not compelling evidence to argue that because Paul's enemies never contested his claims, then their lack of refutation of Paul's writings is sufficient proof for Paul's transformational experience. I repeat an argument from silence is never determinative.

Think how ridiculous the implication is. Let's take an admittedly extreme example. Adolf Hitler wrote *Mein Kampf* in the 1920s. In that book, he outlined his plan to control Germany by making the Jews his scapegoats. To my knowledge, not one single person has refuted the extreme views contained in that book. But that is not because its contents are irrefutable. Rather it has more to do that his views were so extreme that the general opinion was "why bother?"

Furthermore, the fall of Jerusalem at the hands of the Romans made possible the wholesale burning of Jewish texts. Under such circumstances, the argument from silence becomes even more specious.

In the Epistle to the Galatians dated several years before the First Epistle to the Corinthians, Paul's use of the Greek word *ophthe* is enlightening. Examine the previous contexts in which the word *ophthe* is used. It is used in Genesis 12:7 when the Lord appeared (*ophthe*) to Abraham. It is used in the Book of Exodus (3:2) when the Lord appears to Moses through a burning bush. It is used again in Acts (9:17) to describe Paul's Damascus road experience.

The word *ophthe* in the above context relates to subjective experiences as they relate to the ineffable. It pertains to the order of visions.

Is there any doubt that Paul's road experience was a vision? If one reads Corinthians 1:35-58, it should be obvious that Paul goes to great lengths to distinguish the spiritual body from the physical. "The body that is sown is perishable, it is raised imperishable; it is sown in dishonor, it is raised in glory; it is sown in weakness, it is raised in power; it is sown as a natural body, it is raised as a spiritual body" (1 Corinthians 42-44).

Paul goes on to write that the natural body (physical) precedes the spiritual body. "The first man was the dust of the earth, the second one from the heaven." In this important passage what I believe Paul is saying is that we each have a twin nature: body and spirit. The body belongs to Earth. The spirit belongs to heaven.

This is pure Cartesian dualism predating Descartes by over fifteen hundred years. The domain of the spirit is different than that of the body. Flesh and blood cannot inherit the Kingdom of God. Paul's dualism cannot be any clearer,

JM quotes Professor Gundry as stating that the Greek word *soma* "says something about the nature of Jesus's resurrection."[2] As I have mentioned previously, the Jews believed in the general resurrection at the end of time. For Paul, Jesus's resurrection symbolized the end or "the first fruits of those who have fallen asleep" (1 Corinthians. 15:20).

But Paul's distinction between the physical and spiritual bodies remains undisturbed. And when combined with the use of the Greek term **ophthe**, the reference to a vision is unmistakable.

B: On Mark's Account of the Resurrection

JM starts the account by noting that Mark's narrative "goes back to the actual eyewitness."[3] As I've stated many times before if the issue of eyewitnesses is so important to the Christian story in validating the veracity of the historical records, then why is the historical evidence that is allegedly adduced so far short of meeting legitimate empirical criteria? Why doesn't JM understand that believers do not make for strong, objective eyewitnesses? That is why in current scientific research, the paradigm of double-blind studies is the norm.

The absence of testimony by non-Christian sources is troubling. An argument from silence is never conclusive. My point is merely that the retelling of the story of Jesus by believers is tainted and biased testimony. As such, it can never be convincing.

As an example, JM quotes Moreland as saying that Joseph of Arimathea must've been true because if he didn't exist he wouldn't have been mentioned by name.[4] After all, anyone could've checked out the true status of such an individual.

Once again the appeal to silence is implausible. I would ask why Joseph of Arimathea would risk his role within the Sanhedrin to accord a royal burial to a man who was disgraced by his own Council and Roman law. In Mark, we read that "they (the Sanhedrin) all condemned him as worthy of death" (14:63). Why no record of disagreement at this earlier juncture?

Note further that Mark is writing between 65-70 CE. Paul makes no mention of Joseph of Arimathea. Approximately thirty-five years had elapsed since the time of Jesus's death. The population had an illiteracy rate of over 95%. How accessible was Mark's Gospel to the relatively few non-Christians who could read and write? We know that the Gospels were originally written anonymously. It is only in the year 180 AD that the names are given attribution.[5] Within this historical context, the number of Gospels was well beyond the current number of four. We understand the outcome of having four canonized gospels. But the final decision was intertwined with political considerations.

Pertaining to the empty tomb, JM writes the fact that Jesus's tomb was never venerated proves that the tomb must have been empty. Deductive proofs are never conclusive given the ambiguity of the starting premises. However, this is a double-edged sword that Christians would do well to present both sides.

Jesus was allegedly buried for three days and nights. Even if he was raised from the dead, I find the lack of veneration puzzling. The assumption that this tomb was a temporary abode merits some special attention. And yet, even the absence of a marker where Jesus was buried raises some interesting speculation. Could it be that the disciples upon Jesus's arrest fled to their homes as Mark recounts the story? Hence, it is likely that his enemies buried Jesus. Accordingly, the place of his burial was unknown even to his friends.

If you ask me if I believe that Jesus was resurrected, I would reply with a categorical "yes"–with the added caveat that his resurrection was not physical. I do not believe that tradition had anything to do with empty tombs, royal burials, virgin birth, and the like. These are symbols, which were inadequately used to point to a greater reality. I say inadequately because words belong to the world of the mundane. We can never fully describe one's encounter with the Divine through the limited medium of language. I partially agree with Jewish scholar Pinchas Lapide's astute observation that, "In none of the cases where rabbinical literature speaks of such visions did it result in an essential change in the life of the resuscitated or of those who had experienced the visions."[6]

I say "partially" because Paul's experience on the road to Damascus was clearly a vision that transformed Paul completely.

What then can we conclude? For the believer in Jesus, it is my hope that my brief excursion into the historical record will strengthen his faith. In separating the historical wheat from the factual chaff, the resurrection comes down to the irreducible experience of transformed lives. No amount of accumulating research can alter that fundamental reality. Upon this bedrock, the believer can rest his faith. The symbols used to describe the experience will change as the accumulating sands of science yield new truths. But the meaning of the experience can never change.

I'm impressed by such scholars as Gary Habermas who places so much weight upon the disciples post-resurrection behavior.[7] Of the ten reasons cited, I find number three to be the most compelling. Something occurred to transform the disciples James and Paul. That experience in turn had a profound impact upon the development of the splintered movement within Judaism. A religion is governed by deep-rooted traditions. The day of worship is not changed easily. The fact that the Sabbath was moved from Saturday to Sunday attests to the power of this new movement.

Each age will evolve to make Jesus relevant to the current era. The symbols may change. But the symbolical significance is unchanging. Jesus's relevance is especially appropriate because he was an ordinary man that we can all identify with. As the Son of God, his accomplishment becomes impossible to emulate. But as a man, he becomes the conduit to the Divine.

PART II

THE METAPHYSICS OF GOD'S EXISTENCE

Chapter One: Framing the Discussion

According to the philosopher- Immanuel Kant, there are three great metaphysical issues. Does God exist? Is man free? Does man possess a soul? The remaining portion of the book will deal with the first and last questions.

Rather than deal with the definition of God at the beginning, I shall reserve that task for later discussion. For now, I wish to plunge directly into the so-called proofs of God's existence and observe where the journey takes us.

There are at least two arguments that I consider merit further discussion: (1) the Cosmological, and (2) the Design. I don't believe that arguments from ethics or the ontological are strong enough to justify God's existence.

Briefly, the ontological argument started with St. Anselm. It takes the following form.

1. Premise A: If the greatest being exists only in the understanding then,

2. Premise B: It is possible to imagine that being existing outside the understanding.

3. Conclusion: The greatest being possibly exists.

My problem with this argument has always been the first premise. What does it mean to imagine a being greater than any other? What does it mean to say God is perfect or omniscient or omnipotent? Can an evil entity, i.e., the devil, be perfect?

Immanuel Kant—one of my favorite philosophers—took exception with Anselm in the form that existence isn't a predicate, i.e., it doesn't add anything to the concept. While that observation is counterintuitive, I think the objection is misplaced. I would certainly distinguish between one hundred dollars as a thought and one hundred dollars in my pocket. I think the primary problem lies in assuming that an imperfect creature can conjure an image of perfection. How do we define perfection? And what do we do with the problem of evil?

Pertaining to the ethical argument, I don't believe it is necessary to invoke the existence of God to justify ethical and moral principles. In fact, I believe strongly that morality is undermined to the extent religious principles are invoked. Why? Because a free and open society must precede in order to accommodate diverse religious viewpoints. What the Christian believes will be different for the Muslim, Buddhist, etc.

Briefly, without the merit of defending this claim, I believe that Libertarianism can be successful in defending personal rights independent of religious orientation.

A: Cosmological Argument

Science succeeds based upon the principle of determinism. That is, every effect must have a prior cause. Every cause must have an effect. And so on.

I must quickly note that that deterministic model doesn't work well at the quantum level. Hence, I will confine my remarks to the macro-level.

We know that objects in the world do not contain within themselves the source for their own existence. For example, I depend upon my existence on my parents that have gone before me, nutrients, food, etc. Hence, objects are said to be contingent.

All contingent beings depend upon other contingent beings for their existence. We can proceed to an infinity of causes and the conclusion would be the same: all objects and living things are are dependent upon prior causes. But how can we break out of this myriad loop of contingent causes to arrive at a beginning?

If we posit the existence of God, have we offered an explanation? God, would, of course, become the First Cause and transcend the principle of causality.

According to John Hospers, the causal argument is self-contradictory. "The conclusion, which says that something (God) does not have a cause, contradicts the premise, which says that everything does have a cause."[1]

The deist is saying that the universe is not self-contained. The principle of causality isn't sufficient to explain the origin of the universe. By deduction, we must posit a necessary being to start the process of contingent being.

Is a first cause necessary? Why can't we have an infinite regression of causes? Michael Martin in his book, *Atheism-A Philosophical Justification* writes, "Experience does not reveal causal sequence that have a first cause, a cause that is not caused."[2] As an observation concerning the limitation of our knowledge, this statement is a truism. Neither do we find an infinite causal sequence in experience.

We must be careful not to confuse ontologies at this point. In mathematics, we can posit an infinite series of numbers–going backward or forward. For example, in the classical race between Achilles and the tortoise, how is Achilles able to eventually overtake the tortoise's head start and eventually win the race? Assume that Achilles is at point x and the tortoise is at point x+y. Every step taken by the tortoise can be divided into an infinite number of points. How is Achilles able to traverse this infinity of mathematical points and win the race?

The reason why the question can arise is because it mixes ontologies. Ontology is the study of being or "what is." I don't view ontology as a comprehensive whole. The ontology of the world of atoms is different from the ontology of reality as it is lived. The world of atoms is amorphous, colorless, and ethereal. How is it possible for constituent parts to give rise to objects possessing opposite characteristics?

We can't bridge ontologies. Each world has its unique set of characteristics and even language to describe it.

Similarly, the world of mathematical space is different from "lived space," i.e., the space in which we experience the world. We know that in "lived space" Achilles does overtake the tortoise. Every step that Achilles takes has to be measured against the step taken by the tortoise in "lived space"–not mathematical space.

It is my contention that the concept of infinite regress of causes arises out of such confusion. Is it reasonable to say that a causal chain can extend indefinitely backward? The notion of infinity does not occur in the empirical world. Space and time intertwine the world that we inhabit. Even the Big Bang Theory of the origin of the universe suggests a causal beginning.

If we cannot accept the concept of an infinite regression of causes, then what form must the first cause take? A partial list of uncaused causes would include existence, the universe, matter, energy, substance, and God.

Let us take each in turn. According to Nathaniel Branden, "All causality presupposes the existence of something that acts as a cause. To demand a cause for all existence is to demand a contradiction. If the cause exists, it is part of existence; if the cause does not exist, it cannot be a cause."[3]

The problem with this argument is in the use of the term "existence." It confuses the particular with the abstract. The category of **Existence** presupposes something existing. We refer to the existence of object x, . Existence can never exist independently of its referent.

The use of the term in the context that Branden employs invokes what philosopher- Alfred North Whitehead called, "the fallacy of misplaced concreteness." That is, abstract terms are needlessly confused with their empirical referents.

Another example would be justice. The concept of justice is an abstraction. However, we can see particular examples of just acts. We must distinguish between the abstract and the concrete. Abstractions like existence, justice, courage, etc. have a conceptual, disembodied reality. We can only manifest their reality in particular concrete referents.

Hence, I find it meaningless to say that existence is uncaused. Abstractions are the creations of the human mind and have no empirical counterparts outside of it.

The next term I wish to examine is universe. The term "universe" is a collective noun that refers to "all there is." The universe as such doesn't act in a causal fashion but particular things within it do.

I also find this argument to be guilty of Whitehead's fallacy. It gives a concrete meaning, to what is essentially a series of particular events. The term "universe" is an abstract label that facilitates discussion. The problem lies in the claim that the "universe" could be an uncaused.

A similar example may be the term personality. In my earlier days, I wanted to try to correlate how stable personality was over time. I now realize that to understand that question, it is necessary that we decompose personality to its many dimensions.

The origin of the universe through the Big Bang theory stipulates a small number of gases that condense into an unimaginable size. The universe that existed fifteen billion years ago is certainly different from the universe of today. The point is that the particulars can exist without the collective designation. The reverse isn't true. That is, we can understand the particular causal sequence of certain entities. Our conceptual framing of that causal sequence adds little to our understanding of the particulars.

Pertaining to substance, its candidacy as the First Cause is short-lived. Substance can refer to a particular, concrete thing. To the extent that it fits that description then it becomes contingent. It is true that the term "substance" can apply to any material thing. But we have already established that all material things are characterized by contingency.

Next, we come to matter or energy. Since we can transform one into the other, I shall parsimoniously employ the term energy. We can say that energy or God are worthy postulates for the title of the First Cause.

Just as the deist points to God as the First Cause, the atheist can point to energy. I think it is equally valid to say that either energy is eternal, or that God is eternal.

Note that this particular argument doesn't in any way establish the other characteristics that we normally associate with God such as perfection, omnipotence, loving, etc.

My point is that at this juncture both divergent points can be equally entertained. However, while the deist admittedly invokes faith, the atheist allegedly stands on reason. I wish to challenge this assumption.

Cambridge astronomer Fred Hoyle has calculated the probabilities of life arising out of pure chance as being on the order of 10^{40000}. While this figure is very much in dispute, it points to the larger issue that the origin of life is still not settled. In addition, "in the formation of the universe, the balance of matter to antimatter had to be accurate to one part in ten billion for the universe to even arise... There would also have been no universe capable of sustaining life if the expansion rate of the bigbang had been one billionth of a percent larger or smaller."[4]

It is undeniable that the universe is a "delicately balanced harmony of fundamental constants."[5] What is so impressive is the number of coincidences that have come together to sustain life.

The atheist replies that given a large but finite number of atoms and billions of years, a combination is possible to produce life on Earth, as we know it. As far as we know, there may be a thousand Big Bangs taking place throughout the universe. These explosions in turn produce different permutations of which some are capable of producing life.

I find this argument to be a theoretical extrapolation in its purest form. I believe that it requires as much faith as the deist's belief in God.

Hence, I would conclude that at this juncture a certain amount of faith is required for both the atheist and the deist to sustain their respective belief in the First Cause.

B: Design Argument

Let us continue the First Cause argument and extend it out into another realm. We notice that there are certain regularities in nature. In fact, without these uniformities, the principle of induction would be devoid of scientific meaning.

But why does the universe exhibit order? There appear to be certain laws of nature that govern how matter interacts. For example, we can say that it is the intrinsic nature of matter that when two atoms of hydrogen interact with one atom of oxygen, the byproduct is water. I do not believe it aids our understanding to add the premise of God to explain the interaction.

In addition, if we continue the First Cause argument and claim energy as the foundation, it would be equally difficult to explain how energy governs the interaction.

But the laws of nature require a little more explaining. Where do the laws of nature come from? If we follow the Big Bang theory, then we assume that the laws of nature popped into existence at the outset of this cosmic explosion. Conversely, another alternative hypothesis, that the laws of nature are engendered by molecular interaction would seem more farfetched.

The laws of nature seem to be the relatively stable framework within which life arises. It is the organizing matrix without which, life would be impossible.

Hence, two scenarios that emerge look as follows:

1. Energy starts the process through eternal cyclical patterns of compression and diffusion. In turn, these ongoing-chance eruptions give rise to different permutations, some of which are favorable to life.

2. God creates the universe and undergirds it with intelligible order.

Again both positions require a certain amount of faith. How does the Big Bang give rise to gravitation, electromagnetism, weak and strong nuclear forces, earth's particular axis, etc?

The honest answer is that we simply don't know. Reason has reached its outer limits in trying to tackle these questions. Not because we have insufficient data but because these questions are metaphysical in nature.

Hence, science can never provide us with the necessary answers to a metaphysical question. Whether we accept energy or God as the starting point, faith is no less required.

C: The Deist's God

If we assume the second scenario that God created the universe, what can we say about God?

We are certainly entitled, given the two earlier premises to say that (1) God is eternal, and (2) God has some measure of power. What we cannot say is also important. We cannot infer that God is omnipotent, perfect, omniscient, or even personal.

I believe that it is meaningless to ascribe these characteristics to God. How do we define perfection? Is the evil in the world a reflection of God's perfection? How do we recognize perfection in God?

Similarly with the other attributes. I think it is impossible to reconcile God's omniscience and power with free will, Foreknowledge per se doesn't create determinism. It is when foreknowledge is coupled with creation that free will becomes a casualty.

If I design a robot where I can program his actions and know that the program is effective in producing a given outcome, then free will is illusory. To assert anything contrary is to invoke faith.

Can we assign any other attributes to God? The short answer is "no." To the extent we do, we employ faith.

I have always been bothered by the argument that God created us in order that we may worship him. A God that demands worship isn't perfect. A vengeful God is also troublesome. The Christian claims that God is good because the Bible tells us so. Even if one accepted such circular reasoning, there is nothing logically contradictory to the idea of an evil God.

What God did to the Egyptians at the Red Sea is certainly evil from an Egyptian perspective? In (Numbers 31:1-2) we have God commanding Moses to slaughter every Midianite adult male. When the commanders report to Moses that the women and children have been spared, Moses angrily commands that all the boys and women who have slept with man "be killed." In Joshua 10:12-14, we have God delaying sundown by a day in order to help Joshua kill more Amorites.

If you happen to be an Egyptian, Midianite, or Amorite- the God of the Old Testament can hardly be pleasing.

A God that is personal can turn away from any group and destroy it at will. I fail to understand what "all-loving" means under this context. If the idea of a personal God was to create some measure of security, then this concept would be self-defeating.

Furthermore, whose conception of personal are we talking about? Every religion takes a different slant and claims a monopoly of the truth.

D: The Atheist's Conception of God

The deist's conception of creation is much more parsimonious even though it may not explain much. The atheist has to find an explanation for how things originated without the presence of a creator—personal or otherwise.

Let's start with the question: Why is there something rather than nothing? The advent of quantum mechanics has changed our conception of how we view a vacuum. According to physicist James Trefil, "a bit of matter can appear sponta-neously out of nothing; provided that (1) a corresponding bit of antimatter appears at the same time, and that (2) the matter and antimatter come together and anni-hilate each other (disappear back into the vacuum) in a time so short that their presence cannot be directly measured."[6]

This creation process of matter-antimatter is referred to as a "virtual pair." Now in order for this theory to explain the origin of the universe, something must occur to prevent the virtual pair of particles from their predicable annihilation. If enough particles are separated then "eventually enough of them will pop in the same place at the same time to bend the fabric (of space) to start the expansion going."[7]

Under laboratory conditions, the creation of matter and antimatter is always symmetrical. However, according to Davies, it is possible under extreme high-temperature conditions that this symmetry breaks down. Hence, it is possible (i.e., the theoretical equations would allow it) that a slight amount of matter could be created unmatched by its annihilating opposite. This process would account for the conversion of energy. Hence, the transformation of energy into matter could be construed as the Prime Mover which would be tantamount to God.

Just as it is meaningless to inquire as to who made God, it would be equally nonsensical to inquire as to the origin of energy. The short answer is that perhaps, it always existed.

As a theoretical explanation, positing energy as the starting point would be equally satisfying as positing God. However, Davies confounds the problem by supposing the universe could always have just existed. Similarly,I agree that it would be a category mistake to suppose that just because every man has a mother, then the human race must have a mother.[8] Hence, if every object requires a cause, then, according to this logic, it would be wrong to inquire about the cause of the universe.

As I mentioned earlier, these semantic confusions fall under the fallacy of mis-placed concreteness. Terms such as universe, justice, peace, etc. are semantic con-structions, which facilitate discussion. Hence, it would be misleading and incorrect to place terms such as "energy" and "universe" in the same context. Energy has a concrete manifestation; "universe" doesn't. "Universe" is a semantic abstraction; "energy" is not.

But wait, the atheist might argue: Isn't the notion of God an abstraction? After all, we don't observe God in our everyday encounters. What if God is also a semantic construct? I view these as important questions and I will return to them in the next chapter.

But the other confounding variable has to do with quantum cosmology. At the subatomic level, an "individual particle will come into existence abruptly and unpredictably, at no specially designated place or moment." Hence, the principles of causation and that "something cannot come from nothing" appear to be challenged.[9] Let us plunge headlong and see where the journey takes us.

E: Heisenberg Principle of Uncertainty

It is impossible to understand quantum mechanics without understanding the Heisenberg Principle of Uncertainty (HPU). Werner Heisenberg was a German physicist who, in studying the behavior of light, became aware that quantum mechanics imposes a fundamental limitation to the accuracy of experimental measurements. Why should this be so? Light can be broken down as either photons or waves. Anytime you measure something, the measuring instrument will give off light. While in our everyday world, the effect of HPU is negligible, at the quantum level the impact is significant. Hence, the very process of measuring the particle gives it a jolt that will influence its position or momentum—momentum equals mass of the particle times velocity.

Heisenberg discovered that whenever we measure a subatomic particle there is an intrinsic tradeoff between knowing the position of the particle or its momentum. To the extent we know the velocity, we're less certain about the momentum of the particle. Why this limitation? If you want to measure the position of a particle then it is necessary to use light with very short wavelengths. The shorter wavelengths determine the minimum distances with which we can locate a particle. However, because the shorter wavelength has a high frequency, the disturbance upon the system is significant.

Similarly, if we want to measure the momentum of a particle, the only way we can minimize any disturbance is by using low-frequency light. Low-frequency light means long wavelengths. Long wavelengths mean greater uncertainty in the measurement of momentum.

Another law gives the upper limit to the HUP. If we take the energy of a photon—one quantum of light—and divide that quantity by its frequency, we derive what is referred to as Planck's constant. Planck's constant sets the fundamental lower limit on the smallness of things. Like the velocity of light, it is a constant of nature.

Hence, the HUP is related to Planck's constant in the following way:

$$(\triangle P) \times (\triangle M) \approx Pc$$

The change in position (P) times the change in momentum (M) is approximately equal to Planck's constant (Pc). If the change in position is large then to satisfy the equation the change in momentum must be small. The point is that there has to be a tradeoff between knowing the position and momentum to fulfill the equation.

Given this background, I ask: What in HUP negates the principle of causality or that something can come from nothing? Again, the HUP is partially a limitation upon our measurement methodology. I say partially because the dual nature of a photon as both a particle and wave creates intrinsic uncertainties. But I fail to understand why it is valid to give it ontological status.

Furthermore, even assuming that the HUP is valid, why make the leap that it applies to the macro world? We know that atoms at the micro level appear differently than at the level of perception.

What theory allows us to make the transition between colorless, amorphous entities to objects of perception that have the opposite characteristics?

The principle of causality isn't necessarily negated when you allow and acknowledge that a subatomic particle is still subject to statistical probabilities that it will appear in a certain volume of space within some interval of time.[10] But why assume the absence of the causality principle? If a particle is being produced from nothing, why should even statistical probabilities apply? Could it be that the measurement process is disturbing the equilibrium in the system and an undefined energy input is displacing the particle?

I would add that this is a classic example of where scientists are trying to square the circle. That is, if if something can come from nothing,then the principle of causality is itself negated.Then the entire scientific enterprise would be a casualty of that negation.

The bedrock of science rests upon certain self-evident presupposed, meta-physical truths whose negation would collapse the entire scientific edifice. If a particular cause could have a different effect at the same time and place, then how are we to draw patterns to continue the scientific enterprise? If matter can just magically appear out of nowhere, then everything is unpredictable.

Davies distinguishes four characteristics of laws at the macro-level: (1) the laws must be universal, (2) absolute, (3) eternal, and (4) all-powerful (i.e., dictate the interaction of physical systems).[11]

It would be meaningless to apply these laws to the quantum level. And yet, why is the reverse hypothesized to be true? Why explain the origin of the universe as popping out of nothingness? Not only is this not allowed at the quantum level but also it confuses laws that apply to one realm with probabilities that apply to another. Such ontological realms are not interchangeable and it only serves to further muddy the scientific waters.

In their attempt to find substitutes for God, modern cosmologists have had little appreciation of the price paid. There have been two major turning points toward greater acceptance of God: (1) Big Bang theory and (2) the anthropic principle.

Big Bang attests to the principle that creation is a continuing process. The Big Bang hypothesis creates more problems than it solves. For example, the idea of virtual pairs of electrons mentioned earlier is assumed to have existed prior to Big Bang. This is posited not because of any proof, but because in the concoction of any theory, consistency is the key criterion. But if we assume that opposite pair particles come together and annihilate each other, then certain laws of physics echo in the background. But where do the laws that govern opposite pair interaction or infinite compression of matter come from? These laws are assumed to precede the emergence of matter and its interaction.

Despite these complications, let's stay on the same trajectory and ask: Wouldn't separation between matter/antimatter produce rough equivalence between the two? But the amount of antimatter in the universe is "trifling."[12] How do we explain this discrepancy? At this juncture, ad hoc explanations seem to multiply and exotic theories such as wormholes, daughter universes, etc. are involved. But my point is that these explanations are so speculative that they require as much faith as the deist's belief in God.

The Big Bang hypothesis reveals the universe to be much more complicated than we ever imagined. In its wake, we are left awed by the process in which life has emerged despite seemingly insurmountable odds.

This scenario leads directly to the second hypothesis: The anthropic principle. The universe seems to contain an amazing number of coincidences that seem to have "conspired" to produce life. How did the universe know the right number of neutrinos needed to perpetuate the Big Bang? If the strong nuclear force was weaker (by as little as 2 percent) then the atomic nuclei would become unstable and break down. If the strong nuclear force was slightly stronger then "no stable stars could exist nor liquid water."[13]

Consider the weak nuclear force, which is 10^{14} times the strength of gravity. A slight alteration in that force would preclude the formation of hydrogen.[14]

Or take the interplay between electromagnetism and gravity. "Stars are held together by gravity and the strength of the gravitational force helps determine such things as the pressure inside the star. On the other hand, energy flows out of a star by electromagnetic radiation." If the interplay of these forces had been different by a "mere one part in 10^{40}." then stars like our own sun couldn't exist.[15]

Neutrinos are the most abundant particles in the universe. Until recently, neutrinos were assumed to be without mass. According to Davies, recent results suggest the neutrino mass to be in the order of 5×10^{-35}.

To appreciate the delicate balance involved, if the neutrino mass had been slightly different at 5×10^{-34} then "the gravitational power of the primeval background would have caused a drastic alteration in the expansion of the universe, possibly even halting it completely before now."[16]

Why are the fundamental constants so fine-tuned to the formation of life? In Davies's words, "It is hard to resist the impression that the present structure of the universe, apparently so sensitive to minor alterations in the numbers, has been carefully thought out."[17]

The fundamental constants determine the structure of the universe. In turn, the values of the constants are remarkably sensitive within a narrow range. This is a well-established fact within the scientific community. The question that arises in my mind is: How do we explain that the universe is so conducive to life? If we start with the indubitable premise that life exists and work our way backward to the starting point, we can begin to appreciate the fine tuning necessary to explain the origin of life.

Some modern-day physicists posit an infinity of galaxies or parallel universes. The idea is that given an infinity of time, atomic interaction would produce enough favorable permutations to explain the genesis of life. Is there any evidence to support this theoretical posturing? Is there any evidence of parallel universes? What about "billions and billions" of Big Bangs? The short answer is a resounding "no." But yet I perceive a double standard at work here that I find most disturbing.

When the deist replies that God created the universe, the atheist smugly dismisses such pronouncements as simplistic and devoid of any evidence. However, the atheist's speculation, however sophisticated, is taken as grounded upon firmer ground.

It is my contention that both the atheist and deist are operating in the realm of faith. One position is not superior to the other. The atheist may wish to counter that science will eventually explain the universe- independent of any creation hypothesis. As an example, Stephen Hawking and Roger Penrose have speculated that once gravity becomes strong enough then the collapse of space-time into an unimaginable singularity becomes unavoidable.

However, according to this theory, it would be incorrect to argue that this singularity had a beginning in time since time didn't exist prior to the Big Bang. Singularities occur along a continuum in which space-time itself acts as a boundary. Therefore, instead of picturing a singularity as a cone, imagine the cone as rounded off at the bottom. Each point on the diagram is the same. There is no abrupt beginning or end. The universe becomes self-contained.

Is this a superior explanation to what the deist offers? To be sure, the deist explanation explains little in a scientific sense. Hence, the atheist's bar could be set very low.

The problems that I see with these theories are that certain metaphysical assumptions are implicitly involved. It is meaningless, we are told, to talk about causality prior to Big Bang. Cause and effect are meaningful only within a temporal context. But the concept of time emerges only after Big Bang. Hence, to talk about what happened before Big Bang is a meaningless question.

When scientists talk about singularities, they presuppose certain laws and hence, should be presumed guilty of question-begging. Doesn't the fact that matter is being infinitely compressed presuppose certain laws at work? Doesn't the fact of infinite compression imply change? And doesn't change presuppose a temporal context?

In my opinion, as a philosopher, Big Bang singularities merely shift the problem to a higher level of complexity. Any explanation becomes less fulfilling since there is now so much more to explain.

Furthermore, why do we assume that the laws of the universe emerge from Big Bang? The events leading up to this phenomenon presuppose certain laws already present. From whence do these laws come from? If we posit "billions and billions" of Big Bangs then that presupposes further laws. The cycle now become vicious and we have entered an infinite regression.

If we wish to be grammatically correct, we must note that the concept "universe" is an abstract noun. We can posit energy as the prime mover. But that alone is inadequate. Energy seems to behave according to certain universal constraints or laws. Energy doesn't appear to engender these laws. Rather these laws precede the origins of energy and govern its manifestation.

Perhaps this is the final stage of reductionism. The laws of the universe dictate how matter or energy is organized. But once again, we ask: where do these laws come from? The atheist would reply that they have always existed. The deist would answer that God created them. Fair enough! But is one position superior to the other? What if following Einstein's example of the union of space and time, we collapse the concepts of God and universal laws into one. Hence, God would equal the laws of the universe. Are there any inherent objections to such a naked combination?

As long as the laws of nature remained impersonal and indifferent to the affairs of men, the atheist shouldn't care. The deist would also be agreeable since his god was always construed as a watchmaker who winds the universal clock with complete indifference to the ensuing consequences.

Hence, atheism and deism ultimately converge. Can there be any escape from this bondage that perhaps further scientific discoveries could possibly liberate us?

We need to establish the limits of science. Where science ends, metaphysics begins. Science can only thrive under its empirical methodology. If scientific hypotheses are incapable of being falsified, then by definition it is metaphysical.

For example, if I make a statement that the far side of the moon is made of green cheese, this is not a metaphysical statement. It is theoretically possible to experimentally test the truth or falsity of this proposition.

Suppose, on the other hand, I make this statement: Today everything in the universe doubled in size from yesterday. This is a metaphysical proposition. Why? Because it is impossible to set up an experimental design to refute the hypothesis.

Similarly, when we start talking about the origin of the laws of nature, we are in metaphysical territory. We have reached the limits of science. No amount of further research is going to convince us one way or the other. The tools of science are useless in this domain. The only crutch available to us is faith.

As I mentioned earlier, the atheist requires just as much faith as the deist. It is probable that future scientific discoveries will explain the homogeneity of matter throughout the known universe as a consequence of Big Bang.

We can further speculate that at some future juncture the four forces of electromagnetism, gravity, and the weak and strong nuclear forces will become unified under one elegant equation. We may even discover that our theories concerning dark matter are misplaced in their hidden assumption that the force of gravity is uniform throughout the cosmos. But no amount of scientific advancement will help us deal with the metaphysical questions including the origin of the universal laws.

Beyond the boundary of science, lies faith. Reason alone can't penetrate into the metaphysical realm. Ultimate mysteries will not yield their secrets through the power of reason and existing methodologies. But perhaps new avenues might open up new insights.

F: Paradigm Shift

Imagine a world in which all our presuppositions are destroyed. We would suspend belief in ourselves, the world, and certainly, God. First proposed by Descartes in the seventeenth century, in this world anything is possible. God may be an evil genius who might mislead us into accepting the truth of mathematical propositions. Under this scheme, an evil genius, i.e., God could have us believe that 2 + 2 = 3.. How do we arrive at any final truths within this scenario?

Perhaps a paradigm shift is in order. The physical sciences cannot yield any final truths on the existence of God.

Descartes's answer was to assume that he existed. His famous "cogito ergo sum" sought to explain the foundation of his existence. If I doubt that I exist, then I am thinking. To doubt is to think. But thinking requires a thinker. Hence, the more I doubt, the more I affirm my existence.

Hence, I would like to propose a different path. If we could establish that dualism is a better explanation than epiphenomenalism, then everything else will fall into place. That is, if we could prove that consciousness is not a byproduct of cellular interaction, then we would have a clue to something other than matter. That something may be called spirit or soul.

But would the establishment of a soul within a person prove the existence of God? I suppose one could reply that it would all depend upon what definition we attributed to God. But I would propose that the scales of proof would heavily tilt over to the deist's advantage. Imagine the dilemma that the atheist would find himself in. The atheist worldview allows only external matter in motion. Given an infinity of time, everything is possible including Nietzsche's eternal recurrence. But now we find a completely new dimension of reality that seems to defy the common laws of nature. Spirit could interact   in some undefined manner inter-penetrate the physical. The nature of the interaction need not end the inquiry. Just as explaining the "how" of the interaction of gravity with the physical world re-mains a mystery, new hypotheses harbor a paradigm shift in our thinking about consciousness.

There have been reports of people having ineffable experiences while con-sciousness is assumed to be separated from the body. Furthermore, people in such a state recount a remarkably uniform, ineffable experience of seeing a blinding light.

The phenomenon I'm describing is the near-death experience (NDE). I will postpone discussion of NDE until chapter four. First, an important digression...

Chapter Two: God as an Abstraction

In a debate on the existence of God, Kai Nielsen argues the atheist's perspective by noting that God lacks an empirical referent.[1] We ascribe certain characteristics to God such as perfection, omnipotence, etc. But as I argued previously, these characterizations are meaningless.

We are especially guilty of anthropomorphizing God by attributing a personal relationship. When asked to justify the belief in a personal God the Christian will respond that the Bible says so. And how do we validate the Bible? Because it is the inspired word of God. And so the circle becomes vicious.

I don't believe that such simple logic aids in our understanding of God. But it is a legitimate question to inquire if God is mere wish fulfillment. We live in a universe where the planet Earth is a mere speck set against a background of infinite blackness. The universe may simply be indifferent to our needs. Our belief in God may turn out to be projections upon a cosmic Rorschach.

We must keep an open mind and be receptive to reasonable possibilities.

My first response to Dr. Nielsen is noting the state of physics today. Sub-atomic particles such as quarks, muons, leptons, etc. are mathematical constructions and not directly observable entities. The key requirement is that the constructs are consistent with the mathematical equations. Hence, the fact that God doesn't have an empirical referent is not especially bothersome per se.

The introductions of God into this stage of knowing adds nothing to our understanding. The universe yields its mathematical fruits ever so slowly. But it does bear fruit. We can accept as an observable fact that as science continues its inexorable march toward expanding the domain of the knowable , new discoveries beckon.

The introduction of God is useful at the starting gate. Big Bang presupposes certain laws of nature reverberating in the background. At this starting point, physics breaks down. We are now in the realm of metaphysics. Within this domain, accepting either God or the laws of the universe as a given is acceptable. As I argued previously, neither the deist's nor the atheist's propositions are superior to the other.

To go beyond deism and speculate that God is a personal entity takes us into the realm of faith. Within this realm, all subjective beliefs are equally valid.

The epistemological limits of reason determine the starting points. Once the process begins, there appear to be empirical mechanisms that take over. This is the domain of science.

These starting points are problematic at two levels: (1) universal and (2) planetary. At the universal level, we have noted how Big Bang cosmology presupposes certain laws to initiate the process. Similarly, the question of how life began on Earth also assumes certain metaphysical presuppositions.

If an atheist is asked how life on earth started without the presence of a creator, the typical response is to cite the Stanley L. Miller's experiment in 1952. In those experiments, sparks simulating lightning were sent through a flask containing methane, ammonia, and other gases thought to abound Earth's pristine atmosphere. The result was that complex hydrocarbon molecules were produced and eventually, amino acids. Amino acids are the precursors to protein and are necessary to the formation of organic life.[2]

Seems simple enough? So what's the problem here? As Michael Behe brilliantly points out, "The major problem in hooking amino acids together is that, chemically, it involves the removal of a molecule of water for each amino acid joined to the growing protein chain. Conversely, the presence of water strongly inhibits amino acids from forming proteins."[3]

Since three-quarters of the planet is water, proteins had to somehow evolve in dry environments. One theory proposes that amino acids from the ocean washed up on land. The hot surface would heat up the amino acids and would act as a centrifuge in separating the water from the amino acids.

In every experiment done to date, this process succeeds in producing a "smelly, dark brown tar"[4] and no amino protein chains.

Experimental manipulation of different chemical mixes thought to exist at the beginning of our planetary evolution has yet to yield any conclusive theories on the beginning of life. And yet, Stanley Miller's experiments are often cited as proof that the problem has been convincingly solved.

The holy mantra of science is "given enough time." Given enough time anything is possible. But is it really? According to astronomer Fred Hoyle, do we really think that given enough time a tornado passing through a junkyard will produce a 747 aircraft fully built? The standard response is that natural selection substantially improves the chances for life.

There is so much we take for granted! Life on Earth seems to be evolving toward increasing complexity. But this assumes a biological law in the background that propels life toward that end. The theory of evolution displaces the teleological proof. But in either case, where does this principle come from?

It is at this outer boundary that the intellect is powerless to shed new insights. Positing God as an explanatory device is just as valid as stating the laws of the universe have always existed. But the intellect may not be the only way to truth.

Intuitive Knowing (IK)

There is a substantial body of knowledge that relates to subjective experiences of religiosity[5]. I would place intuitive knowing (IK) in the same camp as the NDE. IK is a relatively unexplored mode of obtaining knowledge beyond the usual five senses. Traditionally, IK has been the way of the mystic. Scientific ignorance always precludes scientific scrutiny. But ignoring the issue will not make it go away.

I'm deeply touched but the numerous examples of individuals reporting an encounter with the divine. Either a collective madness is sweeping the planet or a perception that transcends the usual five senses is possible. As I've mentioned previously, we need a new methodology to process these transcendental experiences.

We have ignored them for so long simply because they didn't fit our conventional scientific paradigms. But even within an empirical framework, the implications are revealing. Let's take just one example. An alcoholic had reached the lowest depths of despair. Plummeting from the heights of earthly success, he entered into a spiritual vacuum. In a slow, inexorable, and predictable path he managed to destroy his linkages to his career and family. Isolated from everything that had given him meaning , he continued to drown out the pain of his existence. Caring little if he lived or died, he reduced himself to a homeless wanderer.

At this time, winter had set in. The cruelty of the harsh incipient winter compounded his misery. Survival became the prime directive. In a moment of despair, he allowed himself the luxury to contemplate if life was even worth living. As suicidal thoughts began to invade his weakened mind, he abruptly began to pray. The prayer seemed to emerge from the inner recesses of his psyche asking why, begging for forgiveness. Something was kindled within his soul. In that moment of prayer, he had surrendered himself to a higher force.

In the aftermath, he managed to make amends to his family and most importantly to himself. We cannot fully describe the detailed events of that conversion, but we can clearly see the behavioral change.

To deny the thousands, perhaps millions, of such conversions are taking place throughout the globe is to ignore an important dimension of human understanding. We can speculate what lies at the core. What is the nature of such a life-changing, transformational experience? Are we tapping into some transcendental realm of human consciousness?

What I find astonishing about these kinds of subjective experiences is that we accept them on one level routinely in scientific research in the form of questionnaires, survey results, phenomenological reports, etc. But let the experience include a religious component and we dismiss it as superstitious. Why are poll results valid in one context but suddenly invalid within another? Either the mechanism of self-reporting subjective experiences is valid or it isn't. We cannot have it both ways.

It is ironic that people undergoing these experiences uniformly report these events as being more real than anything ever experienced. But yet we tend to accept the scientifically measurable while dismissing the subjective-no matter how profound.

Pertaining to the argument about God being a mere semantic construction, my conclusion is that in the intellectual realm, at the empirical limits of reason, God is a valid explanatory device.

At the level of intuition, we must develop new methodologies to study the powerful examples of religious conversions where atheists are miraculously turned into believers. If a pill could magically produce such life changing transformation it would be hailed as the greatest discovery of the twentieth century. We can no longer ignore the subjective power and intensity of these experiences. In studying it further, we will begin to know more about ourselves.

Chapter Three: The Near-Death Experience

What is the near-death experience (NDE)? Typically it is an experience in which the individual perceives a life-threatening situation and during which consciousness is split off from the body. While in this conscious state, the individual remains able to perceive events around him including those happening to his body.

What I find interesting about these phenomena is the similarity of the experience among all people across different cultures and religions. The NDE would be much easier to dismiss through a non-spiritual explanation if all the accounts were completely different and could be correlated with certain subgroups based upon such factors as culture, race, degree of religious beliefs, etc. But by present accounts, the atheist is just as likely to have the experience as the believer.

Another interesting aspect of NDEs is the stages that different people report going through.[1] Assuming that these stages are uniform across cultures then the clear implication is that the NDE opens the door to an independent reality.

Phillip Berman, in his book *The Journey Home – What Near-Death Experiences and Mysticism Teach Us About the Gift of Life*, recounts the NDE of Dr. George Rodonaia. Dr. Rodonaia before his NDE held an M.D. and Ph.D. in neuropathology. During an assassination attempt in 1976 by the Russian KGB his car was directly impacted. In his own words, "It all happened in an instant. First, I saw the car coming toward me then I felt it hit me head-on. I estimate I flew about ten meters, landed face down, and then the car ran over me again..."[2]

Dr. Rodonaia goes on to recount the perception of a very bright light. At first, the light was blinding. But slowly his vision seems to merge with the light. During this state, he experienced a sense of peace and joy like no other. He began to see the interconnectedness of life.

He witnessed a panoramic review of his life flashing in front of him. The present became fused with the past and the future. Time became meaningless.

The crucial point I wish to explore about this representative story is its transformational process. Prior to the experience, Dr. Rodonaia was an avowed atheist. After the experience, he obtained a Ph.D. in the psychology of religion and became a priest in the Eastern Orthodox Church. In 1989 he came to America and worked as an associate pastor at the First United Methodist Church in Nederland, Texas."[3]

How can we account for this seemingly miraculous transformation? Can such transformations occur in other contexts such as traumatic events, trances, meditative states, etc.? Can drugs induce similar experiences? To be sure, we must exhaust the physical before we invoking the metaphysical.

Richard Abanes, in his book *Journey into the Light*, has done an excellent job of reviewing alternative explanations for NDEs. I will be drawing from his book in reviewing alternative explanations.[4]

Let me be clear. The NDE is unique in the transformational nature of that experience and in the corroboration of people's veridical perceptions that could only have come from a vantage point different from that of the physical body.

Pertaining to the types of NDEs, Dr. Bruce Greyson has devised a threefold classification: 1)Cognitive, 2) Affective, and 3)Transcendental.[5] In addition, Dr. Pim Van Lommel in a 2001 study listed the following components along with their frequency of occurrence:[6]

Component of NDE	frequency
A feeling of peace and calm	56%
A sense that death was imminent or had occurred	50%
Entering a tunnel or darkness	31%
Undergo an out-of-body experience	24%
Meet, figures, strangers, deities, or deceased relatives	32%
Meet a being of light, or enter into the light	23%
Undergo life review	13%
Encounter a border or limit, the passing of which means certain death	8%

In studying these life changing experiences, I would propose that we work backwards: from the experience to the causal triggers. However, part of the problem in studying NDEs is that the subject may not be fully aware of the relevant triggers. Furthermore, because the experience itself is said to be ineffable, it becomes difficult to articulate all the concomitant components.

It bears repeating that the initial premises concerning the nature of consciousness ,will bias the proposed explanations. For example, if epiphenomalism is in play then causal elucidations will center around the brain.

Or let's take the discussion through another twist. We know that mescaline is a powerful hallucinogen. We know that mescaline intake can produce highly vivid colors and images. What if we assumed that's the way reality really is? Perhaps we have all been prisoners in Plato's Allegory of the Cave. We thought we were seeing the real objects of perception. But maybe, our perceptions are nothing more than Plato's shadows on the cave wall.

Is there an evolutionary advantage to seeing reality more vividly and color-fully? What if our physiological makeup progresses only up to a point where no additional evolutionary advantage is conferred?

I would acknowledge that some of the components of the NDE are engendered through drugs. However, it would still be premature to dismiss the phenomenon as mere confabulations. Why? The starting premise governs the trajectory followed. Suppose we start with the presupposition that the brain is a reducing valve allowing us to filter most of our sensory stimuli to prevent being overwhelmed by our perceptions? Given that premise, the function of drugs may be to expand our filters of reality?[7]

But the fact is that drugs do not trigger the majority of NDEs. Hence, to argue for cause and effect relationships far exceeds any available data. Furthermore, the fact that some NDEs report details of veridical perception would argue against a drug induced artifact. By "veridical" I'm referring to information obtained during the NDE that could not be obtained from the vantage point of the physical body.[8]

In *Journey into The Light*, Abanes goes on to describe the work of Wilder Penfield–the Canadian neurosurgeon. In the 1930s, Penfield electrically stimulated the exposed scalps of his epileptic patients. It appears that electrical stimulation of the temporal and parietal lobes can produce some common NDE elements.

There are two open possibilities that are present: (1) NDE-type experiences are pointing to a greater reality, (2) NDE-type experiences are manufactured solely in the brain subject to the appropriate external stimulus. If one accepts the latter explanation, I offer this challenge: let's compare examples where an individual's worldview was completely transformed as the result of a drug-induced experience versus those derived from non-drug induced NDEs. Show me the scientific studies where a pill can magically transform a person from an atheist to a deist.

A: Other NDE Triggers

Abanes goes on to review other triggers such as anoxia, hypoxia, hypercambia, and even epileptic seizures. First, a few definitions are in order. Hypoxia is a condition in which the cells of the brain are not getting enough oxygen. Anoxia is a lack of oxygen in the brain. Hypercapnia is the excessive buildup of carbon dioxide in the brain.

Again, I can believe that the brain is a sensitive organ which is why evolution went to great lengths to ensure the protective cover of a durable skull. But is the only explanation that all these stimuli are producing confabulations s due to brain stimulation? If the causal link is between electrical and chemical stimulation of the brain and certain elements of the NDE, then the explanation is incomplete. But how do we reproduce the life-changing effect that is the core element of the transcendental NDE?

As mentioned previously, one possibility would be that these stimuli are triggering awareness to new, independent realities. The doors to perception of this realm may have always existed. But our current scientific paradigms have failed us in opening up alternate realities.

Hence, we must understand that, as so often in science, the causal sequence isn't clear. As an example, let's take Penfield's fully conscious patient and examine possible explanations for the reported experiences. The experiences ranged from hallucinations and intense emotional states to mystical, religious experiences.

One simple paradigm would be to posit the causal sequence from the electric probe making contact with the temporal cortex. Under this model, all the subjective experiences would be artifacts caused by the probe

But this interpretation is enabled by the underlying presupposition that brain states produce consciousness. What if the brain is akin to a radio receiver? To continue the analogy, if we manipulate that receiver, then random fluctuations are likely to occur. The causal chain remains the same: probe → temporal lobe stimulation→ changing conscious states. Hence, this causal sequence allows more than one explanation depending on the starting point.

We know that if bodily functions cease then the demise of consciousness inevitably follows. Medical science begins and ends with the body. If consciousness is produced independently of the body, then it operates under a different set of laws that elude scientific scrutiny. Such topics such as consciousness and God are outside the domain of science. But the solution isn't to totally dismiss this possible realm of reality. Rather, I would argue in favor of alternative methodologies to study what science has shunned for so long.

The near-death experience is the first wave of assaults upon our current paradigm of epiphenomalism. But science doesn't change its scientific models easily. Witness the following examples.

One theory proposes that increased endorphin levels disinhibit the hippocampus, as well as lowering the seizure threshold within the temporal lobe, NDEs are hypothesized to be the result of limbic lobe and temporal lobe seizures.

Under this model, rapid physiological changes are thought to account for the subjective phenomenon of the NDE. A traumatic event triggers release of neuropeptides providing cortical excitation.

If I believed strongly that brain states produce consciousness, that presupposition would govern my explanations. Similarly, if I were a dualist, then the NDE would offer a different interpretation.

But can we decide definitively in favor of one model? Medical science will not triumph or fail with either model. As I said previously, the addition of soul or spirit was a dispensable redundancy conveniently jettisoned by Occam's Razor.

Within an empirical framework, we need to examine the psychological changes brought about as a result of the NDE, To the extent that we reproduce or engender those experiences in the laboratory, a new door is opened to further exploration. In all instances, the reality of the subjective experience remains with all its attending implications for the nature of consciousness. Under this paradigm, we accord respect to the meaning and the importance that each individual attaches to this transcendental experience.

There are two particular manifestations of the NDE that wait for a scientific explanation. The first is the claims of individuals who leave their physical bodies while lying on the operating table. If we are ever to transcend the anecdotal evidence, then we must set up an empirical design to validate that reality.

Suppose we advise a select group of subjects about our experimental design. A hospice center would be the ideal environment. A control group from a different setting, say a rehabilitation center could be used with the same individual instructions. In an adjacent room, we could set up a random number generator next to a clock. The objective would be for the individual to report back the numbers displayed on the generator along with the particular time shown on the clock-face.

Let's assume that the subject is able to accomplish this task, would the requisites of science be satisfied? Let's allow the James Randi skeptics of the world to attempt to duplicate the experiment. Speaking for myself, the Uri Geller phenomenon of bending spoons or keys was most easily dismissed when James Randi could duplicate the feat on national television.

The experiment must be foolproof. To the extent it fails to be replicated by a professional magician, then the integrity of the experiment is re-affirmed. A similar paradigm could be used with individuals claiming to achieve an out of body experience (OBE).

Replication is the key to validating the experiment. Other experimenters with different subjects must try to repeat the experiment. The designs will vary. But the scientific methodology must be impeccable.

We must respect the methodology of science but recognize its epistemological limits. The fruits of the scientific endeavor are too powerful to ignore. But we must be open to new realities and dimensions. If indeed, it does turn out that consciousness and the body can be separated, the practical effect on our everyday life will be seemingly inconsequential. We will still have to go to work in the morning. We will still have economic needs. Still pay out taxes. But in the realm of faith, the consequences will be life-changing.

The second manifestation of the NDE that bears further study is its transformational aspect. As John Locke reminded us over two hundred years ago, the brain is thought to be a *tabula rasa*. All of our mundane experiences are etched in the brain. Our experiences in turn produce certain beliefs and attitudes and our beliefs and attitudes loop back upon our behavior. That is, we engage in certain behaviors based upon our beliefs. The atheist doesn't go to church because. such behavior is incongruous with his beliefs. Conflict between our beliefs and behavior produces cognitive dissonance. Dissonance is uncomfortable and anxiety-laden. Hence, we usually tend to avoid it.

Our accepted folklore of the brain producing consciousness is teetering on its foundation . The transformational element of the NDE turns this model on its head. . Furthermore, why the shift toward the spiritual? We would expect to find different attitudes and opinions following an NDE.

On the contrary, we find that the "subject who survives an NDE is irrevocably altered for life."[9] Some claim to have a closer relationship to God. Most individuals become more spiritual, and some, a minority, are affected negatively.[10]

The unique thread that weaves through the NDE is its transformational, unforgettable and life-changing aspect. On this basis alone, it warrants further study.

Perhaps, in the final analysis, it may turn out that such speculation is mere wish fulfillment. Perhaps,in this seemingly uncaring and indifferent cosmos, our existence may turn out to be nothing more than an ephemeral accident, a fluke in the eternal cycle of birth and death,

As our knowledge increases, previous metaphysical questions may find answers. As I stated previously, the issue of God's existence is too big to tackle directly. Rather we must approach God through the inner door bearing the question: Does consciousness exist outside the body?

If we placed the same amount of effort in studying this issue within an empirical framework as we did placing a man on the moon, I believe we could answer the question definitively.

At present, scientists feel very uncomfortable with such words as "spirit," "soul," and "God." Matter or the organization of atoms is, for the materialist, the final cause. But if consciousness can exist outside the body, then a different cause must be operative? But where does the arrow point?

The theory that brain states or cellular interaction produce consciousness starts with a metaphysical presupposition. For all our pride and achievements in the scientific enterprise, we must temper our successes with a large dose of humility.

The German mathematician Kurt Godel in 1931 developed what later came to be known as the **Incompleteness Theorem**. The basic idea that a mathematical system is incapable of being proved or disproved given any number of fixed assumptions. For example, let's take the following statement.

"This statement is false." How can we determine the truth or falsity of this statement? Assume that the statement is true, then its contents declare it to be false. Suppose that the statement is indeed false, then the statement itself is true. The bottom line is such a statement cannot be answered as to its truth and falsity.

Something akin to the Incompleteness Theories is operating in consciousness research. Examine this statement: "The brain produces consciousness." Can we prove or disprove this proposition? We assume that if all brain functions cease, then consciousness is eliminated. But that is analogous to smashing a radio and thinking that all transmissions must end.

But what is the evidence for believing that the brain is producing consciousness? We note a certain correspondence between brain activity and consciousness. We know that most conscious activity occurs during the beta state. Hence, if electrodes could be attached to my brain as I'm writing these sentences, we would expect beta states to predominate.

What I find peculiar about this commonly accepted belief is the intrinsic errors in logic. A concomitance of two events doesn't produce cause and effect. The philosopher David Hume made this plain over two hundred years ago. The fact that brain states are correlated to certain neural activity explains little. Why? Because it would also allow a dualistic theory. Assume that consciousness is independent of the body. We can hypothesize that consciousness uses the body as a vehicle to express itself. Hence,it would be quite plausible to witness concomitant neural activity under this model.

The current theory that the brain produces consciousness is an unprovable assumption. It is in the same vein that man has free will. We believe in these propositions not because they have been proven scientifically, but for pragmatic reasons.

Positing the concept of "spirit" or "soul" doesn't advance the enterprise of science. And the scientific game may be the best show in town. But what if that domain was the tip of the scientific iceberg...

Suppose further that Aldous Huxley's description of consciousness as a "reducing valve" is the proper starting point. Under that model, we can begin to formulate a theory of the psychedelic experience. Commenting on the effects of his own mescaline experiences, Huxley noted how consciousness seems to expand under its effect. It seemed as if a drop of individual consciousness united with the ocean of consciousness. Huxley referred to this as the "mind at large."[11]

Within this scenario, consciousness would seem to be especially empowered to tackle the metaphysical question of God's existence.

Chapter Four:
Consciousness Re-examined

According to current scientific thinking, consciousness is engendered by the organizational structure of matter. The quality of matter is the same. Hence, modern theories on consciousness display a hierarchical arrangement with the neocortex at the evolutionary apex.

Under the guiding force of evolution, matter organizes into separate layers of complexity. Given enough time, different organizational parameters can be engendered. This is the operative theory.

To be sure, within the scientific paradigm, it is the only formal game in town. But are there any gaps in the theory?

Take a common phenomenon like memory. Does memory occupy a physical substrate? Can we establish a point-to-point correspondence between a particular memory and its physiological substrate?

If we follow the work of Karl Lashley in search of the engram–the physiological correlate of memory, progress comes ever so slowly. Lashley's lifelong search for the engram ended in failure.[1]

If memory is not located in a singular engram within a particular locus of the brain, then where is its physical substrate? Perhaps if memory is nowhere, then like a hologram, it may be everywhere within the brain. A holographic image embodies the whole in its parts. That is, we can reconstruct all the data of a hologram from a smaller part. Perhaps the engram is distributed throughout the brain.

What is intriguing about this hypothesis is that Karl Lashley's research with rats involved removal of almost two-thirds of the cortex without any visible memory impairment. The holographic theory would explain that all the information in the removed cortex was contained in the remaining portion.

But this analogy can only go so far. If we remove certain brain structures such as the hippocampus then memory retrieval is definitely impaired.

Let's take another example: consciousness. How does the brain produce consciousness? The simple answer is that we don't know. However, we have faith in the powers of science to yield new answers to age-old questions.

But let us fast forward. We have dissected and examined every iota of brain tissue. Are we any closer to finding any answers? Perhaps the field of artificial intelligence may yet yield certain insights. If every neuron in the brain is compared to a microprocessor, then, by extension, we may be able to produce consciousness in the laboratory

The human brain can contain up to one hundred billion neurons. At the present, we can link up a few thousand processors. But suppose that we could theoretically link up say ten billion of the most advanced) microprocessors. Can we extrapolate what the results are likely to be? Firstly, I think that we can categorically state that the linkage of processors does not engender consciousness. Even if we increase the quantity of processors exponentially, the production of consciousness would remain elusive. In computer jargon, the hardware per se is incapable of producing anything, let alone consciousness.

The hardware needs to be supplemented and complemented with software instructions. The hardware may be necessary but never sufficient.

I believe that this is a powerful analogy that can take us to a new paradigm. We have approached the metaphysical boundaries of epiphenomenalism. The dissection of the brain is complete and exhaustive. A paradigm shift is needed.

We have come a long way from Cartesian dualism. The tremendous advances of medical science yielded a bountiful harvest. If a patient manifests some physical abnormality, say a malignant tumor, we would operate to excise the tumor. Countless surgical operations over the centuries have amply demonstrated the power and effectiveness of medical science. All problems were localized within the hardware. The software was simply ignored.

However, a subtle and silent revolution has gone by virtually unnoticed. The effect of the mind upon the body is indubitable. Our thinking can affect our health, brain states, and even our longevity. The focus of our well-being is at that crucial interface between our minds and bodies. Or between the hardware and software.

The analogy isn't complete. We can differentiate the software from the hardware in the computer arena. However, in the current model of allopathic medicine, the brain is equated with the mind. As mentioned previously, this substantial shift in paradigms grew as the triumphs of medicine multiplied. The ghost of the machine was dead. The machine was the only thing that mattered.

We seem to have come full circle. The "ghost" does matter as much as the "machine." But does the machine engender the ghost?

Certain phenomena cannot be adequately explained within the confines of this model. Much of the evidence is anecdotal because the grip of epiphenomenalism is so complete.

A person starts to pick up the telephone to dial the number of an old friend. The friend on the other line is startled because he too was in the process of dialing the same friend.

Two subjects in the laboratory are linked to EEG machines. One is acting as the receiver. The other is the sender. At the precise moment, the sender sends a message, the receiver's EEG readings show unusual heightened activity.

A comatose person is being operated in a hospital room. Suddenly, her consciousness disassociates from her body. She vividly recalls all the facets of the operation including the instruments used with uncanny details.

There is a disturbing accumulation of evidence that is constantly battering the foundation of our current paradigm that equates the mind with the body. The cracks that are starting to appear can only widen as the evidence grows. What new paradigm can replace epiphenomenalism?

As mentioned previously, what if consciousness is akin to a television set. A television set functions as a receiver in picking up certain broadcasting signals. If the television set ceases to operate, we don't conclude that the signals are no longer being sent. The television set isn't producing the program.[2]

The television set is the body. The signal is consciousness. The two are distinct and separate. How is this dualistic model superior to the existing paradigm?

Firstly, dualism would be able to account for all the near-death or out-of-body experiences. Consciousness is not dependent upon the body. Hence, consciousness can be separated from the body under certain conditions.

Secondly, if the brain is like a receiver, then we may be able to account how different individuals can communicate across time and space. When I pick up the telephone to call your number, your brain may be picking up the same signal independently.

Most importantly, I think that it is fair to ask how the brain produced something so radically different as consciousness. But then again, atoms give rise to objects that are radically different from their constituent parts.

But that's not where the difficulty lies. The brain operates under causal laws. If I apply an electric probe to the brain, it will produce a certain observable effect.

Consciousness is different in that it operates independent of the law of cause and effect. A particular cause will produce a different effect. The key component of consciousness is self-awareness. If I know that you're manipulating me, I can offer a different response than what would be predicted by the causal stimulus. Within the materialistic framework, the chain of cause and effect has produced evolving organisms culminating in *homo sapiens*. Our species is believed to be at the apex of the evolutionary ladder through the development of the neocortex.

However, at the level of self-consciousness, that causal chain is broken. We are no longer chained to the inexorable workings of the causal process. At this stage of consciousness, we are open to make choices. That is, an individual confronted with multiple choices will make unpredictable responses. Determinism breaks down at the level of self-consciousness. The past doesn't equal the future.

But let's assume that we don't wish to concede this premise. Suppose that we allow that the law of cause and effect is still operative at the level of self-consciousness. What are the consequences? In a word, devastating. Under this scheme, it would be impossible to assign individual responsibility. We are all puppets dangling on strings buffeted by forces, which our ignorance hides.

Is determinism superior to indeterminism? Hardly! On pragmatic grounds alone we can reject determinism as being inhospitable to a civilized society. However, pragmatism is not our only ally. We act out our life as we had the ability to make choices. In the course of the day, we make countless choices and we take pride in our competence to do so? What trickery of mind or nature could possibly account for such a grand illusion? If we assign determinism to the realm of objects and indeterminism to the realm of consciousness, we can get the best of both worlds at bargain rates.

Similarly, we can extend this analogy to the mind-body problem. Medical science can continue its dominion over the physical body. However, the body must be distinguished from the soul or mind. Just as Newtonian physics cannot explain macro-phenomena such as light bending around gravitational bodies, epiphenom-enalism cannot explain all the accumulating evidence that points to consciousness being independent of the body.

The warning signs are exhilarating, as they are disturbing. Exhilarating in that a new door is opening up new vistas in our evolutionary development. Disturbing in that a new paradigm shift is always upsetting to the status quo.

In this evolving shift, the cards are stacked in our favor. The model of epiphe-nomenalism—like Newtonian physics—is still valid within a narrow domain. However, in trying to explain such phenomena as the near-death or out of body experinces, it has failed miserably.

Chapter Five: Concluding Remarks

The NDE may be the most significant area of research that will have the greatest impact upon our lives. Religion has been society's primary instrument to inculcate the delay of gratification for the sake of heavenly rewards. Perhaps, our animalistic impulses could only be tamed under the threat of eternal damnation.

Even today, the minority that tyrannizes the majority and commits a dispro-portionate number of illegal acts, is a poignant testimony of the evil that prevails when moral values fail to take hold. It would be a truism to assume that those who wantonly abuse the rights of others are not imbued with ethical principles. Those who abuse the rights of others fail to see the larger picture and the Oneness of existence..

While it is true that the institution of the church has been politicized over the centuries with disastrous consequences. However, it can also be said to have been a powerful force for good.

If we can change the time frames and test the proposition that physical death doesn't mean annihilation, then heaven and hell take on a new significance. To the extent that we establish survival after death, then ultimate responsibility for one's action is reinforced. In the absence of moral values, the level of hedonism is irresistible. Only by knowing the truth about our own spiritual identity, shall we be set free.

Within this context, I find it dismaying to see Christians quibble about the significance of the NDE. Richard Albanes has written one of the best accounts of trying to debunk the NDE phenomenon from a Christian perspective. He writes, "Several biblical passages confirm that there is indeed something within us (i.e., soul/spirit) that not only animates the body but also makes us who we are" (I Samuel 18:1:2, Kings 4:27, Job 30:16, Psalms 42:4, Zechariah 12;1).

I find the quotation of scripture as the basis for refuting the NDE as nothing short of ridiculous. The Christian must necessarily believe in a dualistic theory of consciousness. This is the major point of concession that any practicing atheist would be unwilling to give up any ground. Then how is the NDE precluded from a Christian perspective?

When the soul leaves the body, that is the cessation of life. But what about those individuals who show all the signs of death but are later mysteriously resuscitated? Where does the soul go during this limbo state?

Once again we must examine presuppositions such as biblical literalism that serve only to obscure the reality of individual experiences. Witness how literalism leads to hypocrisy. If a Christian is "born again" or sees visions of Jesus, Mary, or any other spiritual figure, then the truth of this subjective experience will be accepted within religious circles. Let the same Christian report some religious encounter with a blinding light and he will be boorishly dismissed as a new-age hysteric.

Even in the biblical passage quotes by Abanes, I fail to see any particular passage that precludes the NDE. In fact, Ecclesiastes 12:6 supports it. "Remember him—before the silver cord is severed, or the golden bowl is broken; before the pitcher is shattered at the spring or the wheel broken at the well, and the dust returns to the ground it came from, and the spirit returns to God who gave it."

I read this passage well over twenty years ago. At the time the NDE was referred to as astral projection. In the interim, I've read thousands of accounts of individuals separated from their physical bodies while connected by a silver cord.

The belief in biblical literalism is a faith statement. We cannot use the domain of faith to refute the domain of science. As mentioned previously, I accept the validity of subjective experience, especially if its impact is to transform the individual's worldview.

But there is one other point that really bothers me enough to want to elaborate at length.

If the Christian uses his notion of God to fill the gaps in our knowledge, then the materialist uses an implicit metaphysics to get his theory off the ground. The observation that organisms evolve toward increasing complexity, presupposes a metaphysical law not always explicitly acknowledged.

But the "god of explanation" for the materialist is: given enough time, anything is possible. Suppose that a monkey was given a typewriter and allowed to press the keys at random, could the complete works of Shakespeare be reproduced? According to Dawkins, given enough time, such a task is indeed possible.[1]

Dawkins goes on to hypothesize how long it would take for the monkey to type out a simple sentence such as "METHINKS IT IS LIKE A WEASEL." On a truly random basis, the possible combinations would be in the order of 10^{40} times).

However, if we allow cumulative selection, i.e., selectively choosing the right letters as the monkey randomly picks them, then the results would be radically different. Under this scenario, it would take a mere forty-one "generations" to reproduce the phrase.[2]

The obvious question that I would pose is who is directing the selecting and combination of letters? This is a form of question-begging in the extreme. And yet, Dawkins presupposes intelligent design in his attempt to bolster random permutations. The blind watchmaker is not so blind after all.

But I would go even further. Where do these laws of mutation, reproduction, and natural selection come from? In order for evolution to explain anything, we must presuppose certain causal laws. Just as the Big Bang hypothesis presupposes certain universal laws, the theory of evolution demands nothing less.

In the final analysis, the atheist has to surrender to his own faith to fill the gaps of his own incomplete theory.

The invocation of spirit may well be the missing link in the search for ultimate explanations. Science with all its power cannot enter the domain of metaphysics. The methodology of science cannot be applied to the domain of the spirit. Different laws appear to be operative.

Again I return to the question I posed earlier. Where is evolution taking us? A muscle grows best through some resistance in the form of exercise. Similarly, the spirit seems to grow best through the interaction with matter. We grow spiritually as we face the trials and tribulations of everyday life.

The advent of the computer age and the internet promises a new era of Enlightenment. Throughout history, governments have been the greatest suppressors of human liberty. The information revolution is the Trojan horse to all tyrannies. The greatest concentration of power has always resided in government. Hence, all would-be tyrants flocked to the reins of power.

An ignorant child is much easier to control than an educated one. As the people of the world became more educated and the shadows of ignorance continue to recede, a new age beckons. Concerns of the spirit emerge at a certain point in our collective evolution. A hungry mouth cares little about its spiritual identity. The immediate suffering and pain snuff out any luxury in contemplating life's ultimate mysteries.

A revolution in our material existence will necessarily expand our horizons to include the invisible realm of spirit. The dignity of the individual must always be affirmed. Institutions of power must be subservient to the needs of the individual. Our collective spirituality must be acknowledged.

We tend to learn more from our mistakes than when the path is undisturbed. Perhaps that is why we have been given the narcotic of ignorance at our birth. We grow up with little understanding of our spiritual identity. Arguing backward, we can deduce that our ignorance serves some special purpose. If there is a soul within us, then we are part of the divine. It isn't sacrilegious to affirm our true identity. Perhaps like a hologram, the part reflects the whole. When the mystic exclaims the Oneness of Nature, the hologram is revealed.

To understand our common humanity is have to empathy. Hostility and hatred are bred when the focus is upon our differences rather than our similarities.. Crimes perpetrated against another are a function of the failure to empathize and recognize the common identity that we share with any potential victims.

So much has been spent upon weapons of mass destruction. But so little in the tools needed to cultivate love, respect, and empathy for the individual. Governments in this regard have played a shameful role. It has always served the interests of government to fan the flame of potential wars between nations. Governments have had the greatest expansion of their authority during times of war or crisis.

Our elevation in consciousness will entail making government the intended servants of the people and not its *de facto* master. Political structure determines economic freedom. Creative enterprises cannot be forced. We cannot point a gun to our scientists and compel them to think. Prosperity flourishes most within a climate of freedom and respect for the individual.

The government should be the umpire within the social context. It is inevitable that in the course of daily interactions, disputes will arise.

Science must have jurisdiction over its attempts in advancing our knowledge and exploring causal links within its proper domain. For example, we note that a certain diet is correlated with heart problems. Understanding how events are connected together is at the core of the scientific enterprise.

At the limits of science, religion enters. Religion seeks to understand the ultimate questions of God and spirit.

But what are the philosophical implications of dualism? If indeed we can prove that consciousness isn't dependent upon bodily states, the consequences may well be the most revolutionary in the history of the human race. But that's a very big "if." That is why I would encourage scientific study of the OBE and NDE. As mentioned previously, a simple methodology would be to teach the subject to leave his body and read a random set of numbers in an adjacent room. The scientific design must be foolproof. The scientific fruit is too valuable to have it negated by artifacts or experimental bias.

Once firmly established and replicated a new dimension of reality will be opened. We must face the fact that materialism has died along with Communism and all other statist philosophies.

The individual is the crowning achievement of a long, tedious evolutionary process. But matter didn't evolve by itself. In a manner reminiscent of Platonic Forms, spirit provides the shape while matter provides the substance. The spirit uses matter in its evolutionary development.

All individuals are expressions of Spirit. Spirit evolves to higher forms of awareness through interaction with lower densities such as matter. As embodiments of Spirit, each individual is worthy of respect and even admiration. Competition within certain ground rules maximizes efficiency. But ultimately, it will be cooperation born of a common origin and converging upon a common destiny that will bring us home.

Chapter 6: Personal Remarks

The other day I was watching a science discussion on C-Span featuring Stephen Hawkins and other luminaries of science. Someone asked the question, "Why does the universe have laws?" That question struck a resonant chord within me. It is the question that I've tried to grapple within this book.

The answer that the scientist gave was as humbling as it was weak. Humbling in that it shows our basic ignorance about fundamental questions. Weak in that it begged the question. The proposed response went along the lines: The fact that we're here presupposes certain laws without which our existence would've been impossible.

I submit that doesn't answer the question. As I mentioned previously, the Big Bang hypothesis presupposes causal laws. From whence do these laws come?

Nature continues to shed its secrets slowly. We marvel at the complexity of life and speculate about its origins. We understand that matter is subject to the causal laws of this universe. We observe causal regularities. We feel humbled by the immensity of an expanding universe.

In this final section, I wish to speculate how the evolutionary path is unfolding. And the implications for the future of man, woman, and the universe?

Can you imagine anyone protesting the hunting of whales, dolphins, and animals in general at the turn of this century? Can you imagine being concerned with environmental issues such as global warming, pollution, etc? As we continue to expand our consciousness, we will be drawn more toward what unites us rather than what divides us.

Our collective consciousness is dawning upon a new threshold. A paradigm shift is emerging. Within this model, we must pay homage to the things of the spirit and body.

The success of the medical model can only take us so far. The limits of that frontier are before us. We can dissect the brain until eternity and a viable model of consciousness will elude us.

We can string together a million microprocessors and consciousness will fail to emerge.

We can manipulate and simulate all the known variables at the beginning of our planet, and we still will not be able to propagate life beyond a few rudimentary levels.

There is a crucial missing variable in our equations. The missing X we can call spirit. Spirit is the operative principle that pervades the universe and gives form to matter. The universe is alive! Everything is changing. From the unripe banana on my table to the bacteria and viruses all around us, everything is evolving. You're not the same person you were yesterday.

Matter in motion cannot account for the manifest diversity. How does evolution "know" to proceed in a direction of increasing complexity while entropy commands the opposite direction in the physical domain? How does the giraffe evolve to that particular form of an elongated neck? Would strong hind legs that enhance jumping abilities be more adaptive? And couldn't it be argued that the giraffe's long neck is maladaptive in that it makes it visible to its enemies?

The effect of evolution at the macro level is indubitable. It is reasonable to assume that through better diet, health, exercise, and behavior that a species can evolve within certain parameters.

The problem is explaining the transition from one species to another. Or as Richard Dawkins states, "The biologist's problem is the problem of complexity. The biologist tries to explain the workings, and the coming into existence, of complex things, in terms of simpler things."

An implicit metaphysics undergirds this seemingly simple proposition: Why do we assume that things are moving toward being more complex? A biologist may respond this is merely an empirical observation. But this presupposes a biological causal mechanism. Where does this principle or law come from?

If life started from unicellular organisms, it can only move in one direction if life is to evolve. Fair enough? But what accounts for the increasing complexity? If the watchmaker is truly blind, then life could have been snuffed out at any level.

"Well, we are here, aren't we" may well be the rallying cry of the biologist. But like the model of epiphenomenalism, the raw data remains incomplete. As we continue to push the limits of science, we will necessarily enter the domain of faith. In looking backward, we can marvel at the long evolutionary road that we have traveled and have a greater appreciation for the teleological trajectory of an expanding consciousness.

FOOTNOTES

PART I

CHAPTER 1

1.   Wilson, AN, *Jesus: A Life*, (New York: W.W. Norton and Company, 1992), 88.

2.   McDowell, Josh and Bill Wilson, *He Walked Among Us*, (Nashville: Thomas Nelson Publisher, 1993), 40.

3.   McDowell, Josh, *Evidence that Demands a Verdict, Vol I & II*, (Nashville: Thomas Nelson Publishers, 1979).

4.   Mack, Burton Mack, *Who Wrote the New Testament?*, (San Francisco, Harper Collins Publishers, 1995), 4.

5.   Ibid., 4-5.

6.   Sanders, EP, *The Historical Figure of Jesus*, (New York: Penguin Books, 1993), 57.

7.   Mack, Burton, op. cit., 7.

8.   Sanders, EP, op. cit., 64.

9.   Ibid., 64.

10.   Spong, John Shelby, *Liberating the Gospels*, (New York, Harper Collins Publishers, 1996), 41.

11.   Ibid., 102.

12.   Ibid., 125.

13.   Ibid., 101.

14,   Spong, John Shelby, *Rescuing the Bible from Fundamentalism (RBF)*, (New York: Harper Collins Publishers, 1991), 171.

15.   Crossan, John Dominic , *Jesus: A Revolutionary Biography*, (New York: Harper Collins Publishers, 1994), 145.

16.   Ibid., 145.

17.   Keller, Werner, *The Bible as History*, (New York: Bantam Books, 1980), 391.

18.   Spong, John Shelby, *Liberating the Gospels* , op. cit., 19.

19.   Ibid., 20.

20.   Sanders, EP, op. cit., 23.

21. Crossan, John Dominic, op. cit., 25.

22. Ibid., 25.

23. Mack, Burton, op. cit., 37.

24. Spong, John Shelby, *Resurrection: Myth or Reality (RMR)*, (New York: Harper Collins Publishers, 1994), 9.

25. Ibid., 9.

26. Sanders, EPop. cit., 240-241.26.

27. Ibid., 10-11.

28. Blomberg, Craig, *The Historical Reliability of the Gospels*, (Downers Grove, III: Intervarsity Press, 1987), 53.

CHAPTER 2

1. Dunn, James D.G., *The Evidence for Jesus*, (Louisville: Westminster Press, 1985), 70.

2. Spong, John Shelby, *Resurrection: Myth or Reality (RMR)*, op. cit., 54.

3. Jesus Seminar, *The Five Gospels*, (New York: Polebridge Press, 1993), 93.

4. Funk, Robert, *Honest to Jesus: Jesus for New Millenium*, (San Francisco: Harper, 1997).

5. Ibid., 240-241.

6. Ibid.,241

7. Sheehan,Thomas, *The First Coming*, (New York: Random House, 1986), 193.

CHAPTER 3

1. *Quest Study Bible: New International Version*, (Grand Rapids: Zondervan Corp, 1994), 1386.

2. Spong,John Shelby, Liberating The Gospels, op.cit., 216-217.

3. Jesus Seminar, *The Five Gospels*, op. cit., 93.

4. Sanders, EP,op. cit., 240-241.

5. Ibid., 241.

6. Sheehan,Thomas , *The First Coming*, (New York: Random House, 1986), 193.

7. Ibid., 187.

8. Ibid., 187.

9. Ibid., 193.

10. Ibid., 198.

11. Ibid., 198.

12. Ibid., 199.

13. Spong, John Shelby, *Resurrection: Myth or Reality*, op. cit., 124.

14. Ibid., 124.

CHAPTER 4

1. Spong, John Shelby , *Born of A Woman (BW)*, (New York: Harper Collins Publishers, 1992), 75.

2. Brown,Raymond E., *The Birth of the Messiah*, (Garden City: Doubleday).

3. Sanders, EP.op. cit., 272.

4. Ibid., 273.

5. Sheehan, Thomas, op. cit., 198.

6. Crossan, John Dominic, op. cit., 137.

7. Ibid., 138.

8. Ibid., 143.

9. Grant, Michael, *Jesus: An Historian's Review of the Gospels*, (New York: Charles Scribner's Sons, 1977.

10. Mack, Burton, op. cit., 237.

11. Ibid., 233

CHAPTER 5

1. Funk, Robert and Hoover, Roy, Jesus Seminar, The Five Gospels, Polebridge Press, 1993.

CHAPTER 7

1. Spong, John Shelby , *Resurrection: Myth or Reality*, op. cit., 53-55.

2. Ibid., 233-260.

3. Crossan, John Dominic , *Jesus: A Revolutionary Biography*, op.cit., 190.

4. Sanders, EP , *The Historical Figure of Jesus*, op.cit., 280.

5. Ghandi, Mohandas , *Autobiography: The Story of My Experiments with Truth*, (Dover Publications, 1983).

6. Spong, John Shelby , *Why Christianity Must Change Or Die*, (New York: Harper Collins Publishing, 1998).

7. Schillebeeckx, Edward, *Jesus: An Experiment in Christology*, (William Collins Sons and Co., 1979).

8. Spong, John Shelby Spong, *Resurrection:Myth or Reality*, op.cit., 287-293.

9. Crossan, John Dominic, *Jesus: A Revolutionary Biography*, op.cit., 124-127.

10. Ibid., 124-127.

11. Spong, John Shelby, *Resurrection: Myth or Reality*, op.cit., 239.

12. Brown, Raymond , op. cit.

13. Ibid., 1240-1250.

14. Spong, John Shelby, Resurrection: Myth or Reality, op.cit,

CHAPTER 8

1. Berman, Phil, *The Journey Home*, (New York: Pocket Books, 1996), 125.

CHAPTER 9

1. McDowell,Josh and Bill Wilson, *He Walked Among Us*, op. cit.

2. Ibid., 41-42.

3. Ibid., 88.

4. Ibid., 88.

5. Ibid., 113.

6. Ibid., 118.

7. Crossan, John, *Jesus: A Revolutionary Biography*, op.cit., 164.

8. Ibid., 167.

9. Spong, John Shelby, *Born of a Woman*, op. cit., 143.

10. McDowell, Josh and Bill Wilson, *He Walked Among Us*, op. cit., 208.

11. Sanders, EP, *The Historical Figure of Jesus*, op. cit., 20.

12. McDowell Josh and Bill Wilson, op. cit., 201.

13. Ibid.

14. Deissman, Adolph, *Light from the Ancient East*, (New York: George H. Doran, Co., 1927), 201.

15. Ibid., 271.

16. McDowell, Josh and Bill Wilson, op. cit., 200-201.

17. Ibid., 208.

18. Crossan, John Dominic, *The Historical Figure of Jesus*, op. cit., 357.

19.   Ibid., 357-355.

20.   Ibid., 357-358.

21.   Funk, Robert , *A Credible Jesus: Fragments of a Vision*, (Santa Ross: Polebridge Press, 2002), 94.

22.   Sanders, EP, *The Historical Figure of Jesus*, op. cit., 20-30.

23.   Crossan, John Dominic, *Jesus: A Revolutionary Biography*, op.cit., 82.

CHAPTER 10

1.   McDowell Josh and Bill Wilson, op. cit., 280.

2.   Ibid., 280.

3.   Sanders, EP, op. cit., 64.

4.   McDowell, Josh and Wilson, Bill op.cit.,281

5.   Sanders, EP, *The Historical Figure of Jesus*, op. cit., 64.

6.   Lapide, Pinchas, *The Resurrection of Jesus: A Jewish Perspective*, (Augsburg Publishing House, 1983), 126.

7.   Habermas, Gary R, The Historical Jesus, Ancient Evidence for the Life of Christ, College Press Publishing Company.Joplin,MO,1996.

PART II

CHAPTER 1
FRAMING THE DISCUSSION

1.   Smith, George H., *Atheism: The Case Against God*, (Buffalo: Prometheus Books, 1989), 239.

2.   Martin, Michael, *Atheism: A Philosophical Justification*, (Philadelphia: Temple University Press, 1990), 97.

3.   Smith, George H., op. cit., 240.

4.   Moreland, JP and Kai Nielsen, *Does God Exist?*, (Buffalo: Prometheus Books, 1993), 35.

5.   Ibid., 35.

6.   Trefil, James, *The Edge of the Unknown*, (New York: Houghton Miffin Co., 1996), 9.

7. Ibid., 20.

8. Davies, Paul, *God and the New Physics*, (New York: Simon & Schuster, 1992), 82-83.

9. Ibid., 35.

10. Davies, Paul, *The Mind of God*, (New York: Simon & Schuster, 1992), 82-83.

11. Davies, Paul, *God and the New Physics*, op. cit., 28.

12. Ibid., 187-188.

13. Ibid., 187-188.

14. Davies, Paul, *The Accidental Universe*, (New York: Cambridge University Press, 1982), 61.

15. Davies, Paul, *God & The New Physics*, op.cit. pg.195.

16. Ibid., 161.

17. Ibid., 189.

CHAPTER 2

GOD AS AN ABSTRACTION

1. Moreland, JP and Kai Nielsen, op. cit., 49-56.

2. Miller, Stanley, The Origin of Life on Earth, Denver, CO: Prentice Hall, 1974

3. Michael Behe, *Darwin's Black Box*, (New York: The Free Press, 1996), 169.

4. Ibid., 120

5. Alston, William P., *Perceiving God*, (Ithaca: Cornell University Press, 1991).

CHAPTER 3

THE NEAR DEATH EXPERIENCE

1. Kason, Yvonne and Teri A. Digler, *Further Shore*, (Toronto: Harper Collins Publishers, 1994), 62-64.

2. Berman, Phil, *The Journey Home*, (New York: Pocket Books, 1996), 33.

3. Ibid., 30-35.

4. Abanes, Richard, *Journey into the Light*, (Grand Rapids, Baker Books, 1996).

5. Greyson, Bruce and Janice Miner Holden, The Handbook of Near Death Experiences, Santa Barbara, CA: Praeger Publishing, 2009.

6. Lommel, Van Pim, Consciousness Beyond Life, San Francisco, CA:

Harper One, 2011.

7.   Huxley, Aldous, *The Doors of Perception*, (New York: Harper and Row, 1956), 26.

8.   Rivas, Titus, Anny Dirvin, and Rudolph Smit, *The Self Does Not Die*, (Durham: IANDS, 1913).

9.   Morse, Melvin, *Transformed By the Light*, (New York: Ballantine Books, 1992), 243.

10.   Ring, Kenneth, *The Omega Project*, (New York: William Morrow & Co., 1992), 183.

11.   Huxley, Aldous, op.cit., 26.

CHAPTER 4

CONSCIOUSNESS RE-EXAMINED

1.   Lashley, Karl, *Mechanisms and Intelligence: A Quantitative Study of Injuries to the Brain*, (Maple Grove,MN:Hafner Publishing, 1964).

2.   Alexander, Eben, *Proof of Heaven*, (NY,NY:Simon and Schuster, 2012).

CHAPTER 5 - CONCLUDING REMARKS

1.   Dawkins, Richard, *The Blind Watchmaker*, (New York: WW Norton & Co., 1987), 15.

2.   Ibid., 15.

CHAPTER 6- PERSONAL REMARKS